Rethinking Migration and Return in Southeastern Europe

This book provides an important new analytical framework for making sense of return, remigration, and circular mobility, conceptualising them as different phases of a wider migration process.

Using an in-depth case study of Albania and its two main destination countries, Italy and Greece, the book demonstrates that instead of being viewed as a linear path between origin and destination, migration should be seen as a segmented or cyclical pattern that may involve several localities and more than two countries. Characterized by important previous historical, social, economic, and political linkages, geographical proximity, but also high migration volatility and sustained flows in either directions, Albanian migration to Italy and Greece offers an optimal case study for analysing complex return, reintegration, and mobility processes. While interesting as a unique regional migration system, the lessons learned cast light on important migration and mobility dynamics that are relevant for labour migration in Europe, also from other important migrant origin countries in the EU's neighbourhood such as for instance Morocco or the Ukraine.

This rich theoretical and empirical study will be of interest to researchers within European studies and migration studies, as well as providing a useful contribution to policy debates on how to govern return migration, reintegration, and circular migration.

Eda Gemi is Senior Lecturer at the University of New York Tirana.

Anna Triandafyllidou holds the Canada Excellence Research Chair in Migration and Integration at Ryerson University, Toronto, Canada. She is Editor-in-Chief of the *Journal of Immigrant and Refugee Studies*.

Routledge Research on the Global Politics of Migration

Rethinking Security in the Age of Migration
Trust and Emancipation in Europe
Ali Bilgic

Citizenship, Migrant Activism and the Politics of Movement
Peter Nyers and Kim Rygiel

Migration and Insecurity
Citizenship and Social Inclusion in a Transnational Era
Niklaus Steiner, Robert Mason, and Anna Hayes

Migrants, Borders and Global Capitalism
West African Labour Mobility and EU Borders
Hannah Cross

International Political Theory and the Refugee Problem
Natasha Saunders

Calais and its Border Politics
From Control to Demolition
Yasmin Ibrahim and Anita Howarth

Liquid Borders
Migration as Resistance
Edited by Mabel Moraña

Rethinking Migration and Return in Southeastern Europe
Albanian Mobilities to and from Italy and Greece
Eda Gemi and Anna Triandafyllidou

Rethinking Migration and Return in Southeastern Europe

Albanian Mobilities to and from Italy and Greece

Eda Gemi and Anna Triandafyllidou

First published 2021
by Routledge
2 Park Square, Milton Park, Abingdon, Oxon OX14 4RN

and by Routledge
52 Vanderbilt Avenue, New York, NY 10017

Routledge is an imprint of the Taylor & Francis Group, an informa business

© 2021 Eda Gemi and Anna Triandafyllidou

The right of Eda Gemi and Anna Triandafyllidou to be identified as authors of this work has been asserted by them in accordance with sections 77 and 78 of the Copyright, Designs and Patents Act 1988.

All rights reserved. No part of this book may be reprinted or reproduced or utilised in any form or by any electronic, mechanical, or other means, now known or hereafter invented, including photocopying and recording, or in any information storage or retrieval system, without permission in writing from the publishers.

Trademark notice: Product or corporate names may be trademarks or registered trademarks, and are used only for identification and explanation without intent to infringe.

The Open Access version of this book, available at www.taylorfrancis.com, has been made available under a Creative Commons Attribution 4.0 license.

British Library Cataloguing-in-Publication Data
A catalogue record for this book is available from the British Library

Library of Congress Cataloging-in-Publication Data
Names: Gemi, Eda, author. | Triandafyllidou, Anna, author.
Title: Rethinking migration and return in Southeastern Europe : Albanian mobilities to and from Italy and Greece / Eda Gemi and Anna Triandafyllidou.
Description: Abingdon, Oxon ; New York, NY : Routledge, 2021. | Series: Routledge research on the global politics of migration | Includes bibliographical references and index.
Identifiers: LCCN 2020048793 (print) | LCCN 2020048794 (ebook) | ISBN 9780367361785 (hardback) | ISBN 9780429344343 (ebook)
Subjects: LCSH: Return migration--Albania. | Albania--Emigration and immigration. | Italy--Emigration and immigration. | Greece--Emigration and immigration.
Classification: LCC JV8296 .G46 2021 (print) | LCC JV8296 (ebook) | DDC 304.8094965--dc23
LC record available at https://lccn.loc.gov/2020048793
LC ebook record available at https://lccn.loc.gov/2020048794

ISBN: 978-0-367-36178-5 (hbk)
ISBN: 978-0-429-34434-3 (ebk)

Typeset in Times New Roman
by Taylor & Francis Books

Contents

List of illustrations		vi
Preface		vii

1	Rethinking return, reintegration, and mobility in southeastern Europe	1
2	Setting the analytical framework: Reconceptualizing return, reintegration, and mobility	11
3	Return mobilities of first-generation Albanians: Reconciling the rupture of disintegration and negotiating the future	41
4	Return mobilities of the second generation: Between disintegration and hybrid identities	83
5	A typology of return, reintegration, and onward mobility	124

List of interviewees returned from Italy, 2014–2017	137
List of interviewees returned from Greece, 2014–2017	139
Second-generation interviewees, Italy and Greece, 2017	142

Index	145

Illustrations

Figure

1.1 The migration space — 4

Tables

1.1 List of interviews, 2014–2017 — 6
3.1 Socio-demographic profile of returnees, 2014 — 43
3.2 Socio-demographic profile of returnees, 2017 — 44
3.3 Socio-demographic profile of second-generation returnees, 2017 — 47
5.1 Typology of return migration, re-integration, and mobility — 134

Preface

This book marks a 15-year collaboration and friendship that started at the seminar room of the Hellenic Foundation for European and Foreign Policy (ELIAMEP) when Eda started working at the EU-funded project POLITIS, on the civic participation of migrants in EU countries as one of our country experts. That was back in 2005. This collaboration has developed over several research projects, and has continued even when we both moved on to new jobs and new responsibilities, and also new geographical destinations. The origins of this book lie in our joint reflections on what drove many Albanian families during and after the most difficult years of the Greek financial crisis to return to Albania and what happened after this return. Did they stay? Did they manage to adapt? Did they move on? These questions became pressing empirical and policy questions as the crisis continued, and as our ongoing work in the context of the METOIKOS project (funded by DG Home) and the IRMA project (funded by the Greek Secretariat for Research) showed that there was a substantial and continuous return flow from both Italy and Greece to Albania. Almost ironically, both of us have been 'return migrants' in our respective countries of origin, Albania and Greece, and know first-hand some of the dilemmas, challenges as well as opportunities that this involves. We have also both been involved in onwards mobility and remigration.

Work for this book started in 2014 and continued till 2017 thanks to the financial support of the Global Governance Programme of the European University Institute in Florence, Italy, where Anna had moved to in 2012. This limited funding made it possible for Eda to travel back to Albania and conduct interviews with returnees. As the work progressed, it became clear that it was important to include not only first-generation returnees, but also those that are not returning but rather moving back to their parents' home country, notably the second generation. We were thus able to delve deeper into their experiences, and also to the academic literature, and identify some of the missing links between return, reintegration, and onward mobility, which this book seeks to fill.

This research was completed in the summer of 2020, under a pandemic lockdown, thanks to some additional funding support from the Canada Excellence Research Chair in Migration and Integration Program of Ryerson University. One might argue that the many seas that this book has travelled reflect the transnational mobility experiences of our interviewees. We are grateful to our respective families for their patience and support during these years as research work often inundates what should be 'free time' and 'family time'. This book is dedicated to our children, young cosmonauts of this mobile world.

Eda Gemi, Athens/Tirane
Anna Triandafyllidou, Toronto
20 October 2020

1 Rethinking return, reintegration, and mobility in southeastern Europe

Introduction

This book studies the return, remigration, and circular migration of Albanian citizens towards Italy and Greece in the 2010s. It develops a new analytical framework for making sense of return, remigration, and circular mobility by conceptualizing them as different phases of a wider migration process. We disentangle reintegration from return and question whether and how successful reintegration can discourage or encourage remigration, depending on the opportunity structure and motivations of the migrant. This book is inscribed in an innovative strand of the literature that brings together the study of return, reintegration, and remigration with that of circular migration – an understudied but much-discussed phenomenon in itself (Triandafyllidou 2013) – showing how these different flows are part of a wider, complex migration pattern. Likewise, this study departs from linear concepts of migration between an origin and a destination and privileges an understanding of migration as a segmented or cyclical pattern that may involve several localities and more than two countries (see also Nadler et al. 2016; Triandafyllidou 2017a; Gemi, 2017).

Our study focuses on a triangular migration system that brings together Albania and its two main destination countries, notably Italy and Greece. This migration system is characterized by important previous historical, social, economic, and political linkages, geographical proximity but also high migration volatility and sustained flows in either direction. As such it offers an optimal case study for analysing complex return, reintegration, and mobility processes. We argue that while interesting as a unique regional migration system, the case of Albania, Italy, and Greece can cast light on important migration and mobility dynamics that are relevant for labour migration in Europe from other important migrant origin countries in the EU's neighbourhood such as Morocco or Ukraine.

The book draws on extensive qualitative research, notably 67 qualitative interviews conducted in several Albanian cities during the period 2014–2017. Our approach focuses on the micro-level, notably on how migrants make sense of their migration projects, how they deal with uncertainty and changing socio-economic conditions, and how they take decisions and mobilize resources whether to return, remigrate, reintegrate, or circulate. Our qualitative micro-level investigation is informed by our analysis of the macro-level factors at origin and destination (employment, household structure, wider economic conditions, and relevant labour, migration and welfare policies), and the meso-level elements (specific contextual factors such as networking with co-ethnics and locals at destination and with family and friends at origin, professional networks, access to support by civil society or state institutions). This introductory chapter briefly places the book in the wider scholarly literature framework and explains why studying the migration between Albania, Italy, and Greece offers an interesting case study. The chapter concludes by outlining the book's structure and contents.

Return, reintegration, and onward migration as one continuum

Return migration has been a key concept in migration studies in recent times, whether to discuss irregular migration and the (forced or voluntary) return of illegally staying migrants or to analyse the potential of diasporas, remittances, and transnational mobility. Return was initially conceptualized as the endpoint of the migration cycle (Gmelch 1980). However more recent studies have pointed to the complex character of return, reintegration, and the dynamics of remigration and circulation (Kuschminder 2017a, 2017b; Triandafyllidou 2013) suggesting that return should be seen as an episode in the wider migration cycle.

Thilo et al. (2016) in particular have investigated the return and reintegration patterns of European migrants within Europe, including the return conditions of non-EU nationals to countries located in the European geographical periphery, notably the Balkans, Eastern Europe, the Caucasus, and Turkey. They explore the motivations for return and the concept of 'return readiness' which the authors consider basic components in the analysis of the dynamics and patterns of reintegration. Our study seeks to treat both reintegration and remigration or onward migration as part of one fluid continuum of migration rather than treating reintegration and remigration as two opposite poles. We seek to disentangle reintegration from return and show how successful reintegration can discourage as well as encourage remigration, using our insights from the specific migration system that brings together Albania and its two main destination countries, notably Italy and Greece.

Despite the wealth of research pointing to the complex realities of return – prepared, voluntary, or abrupt and forced return, by choice, by opportunity, or by necessity – policy thinking has been fixed on two opposed views of return. One is return as 'success': migrants have achieved their aims, completed their project, and are returning to their 'home' country. The second is return as failure: migrants are forcibly (or voluntarily) returned to their country of origin (or last country of transit) because they do not have the right to stay. In the policy discourse, return is somehow the opposite of mobility and ambivalence: it brings the migrant back to their 'natural' situation of being in their 'homeland' where they 'belong'; or, it re-establishes order and security as it forcibly removes those who do not have the right to reside in a given destination country. The perspective adopted in this book is different, and points to the dynamic nature of return migration.

Significant attention has been paid to successful return and reintegration. For those wishing to return and often bringing with them financial and social capital, return is seen as part of a migration and development nexus (King 2017; Kuschminder 2017a). Thus, successful reintegration is key to their potential contribution to the country of origin through investment, new ideas, or trade and business networks. For those who are forcibly returned, reintegration is also critical as it is expected to discourage remigration, particularly irregular remigration. In either case the intention of staying in the country of origin and not emigrating again is seen as crucial to the successful return often conflating reintegration success with intentions to emigrate, presupposing that someone who is successfully reintegrated would not wish to leave again (Kuschminder 2017b).

Our study builds on these insights and particularly recent research on return and remigration in southeastern Europe (Loizou et al. 2014; Maroukis and Gemi 2013; King 2018) with a view to further developing an analytical framework within which to make sense of return in a context of increased and more fluid migration in twenty-first-century Europe (Triandafyllidou 2017b). We conceptualize return as part of the wider mobility process in which the migrants engage. Return is seen as one dot in a non-linear course that may include multiple emigration and return sections as well as remigration (whether to the same destination country or to third countries). In our analytical framework reintegration is not necessarily about sedentariness; it is not about staying put and not emigrating again. Rather we conceptualize preparedness (for return) and reintegration as two processes that 'frame' return since preparedness precedes it and reintegration follows it and in that sense condition further decisions of staying in the country of origin or remigrating. We see reintegration as a separate dimension from intentions of remigration. A successful reintegration may be a precursor to a new migration project rather than a factor for staying as it allows the migrant to gather both material and social resources. At the same time a failed reintegration may be a factor discouraging remigration because of lack of resources – or, of course, it may be a driver for remigration because of the lack of prospects at the country of origin. In other words, the relationship between return, reintegration, and remigration is more complex than has been argued thus far. It is this new element that our study sheds light on.

We propose a migration space that is organized along two dimensions: mobility vs immobility as a spatial dimension of staying or moving, and a temporal dimension that is a continuum between a short-term/temporary and long-term/settled perspective (Figure 1.1). Both mobility (emigrating and remigrating, migrating towards a new destination, circulating between two countries) and immobility (staying and returning) can be temporary or long term.

In order to operationalize and test our framework, we place our analysis of the different aspects of mobility and immobility within a migration system – notably a set of countries sharing important social, economic, cultural, historical, and even political ties and that may also have experienced migratory movements in the past (see also Triandafyllidou and Hatziprokopiou 2013), in this case Albania, Italy, and Greece.

Our approach focuses on the agency of the migrant and on what migrants 'do' to address the hardship they face, how they seek to use or circumvent policies, and how they mobilize both material and social

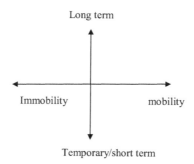

Figure 1.1 The migration space

resources (Triandafyllidou 2017a) to prepare for return (Cassarino 2014), to reintegrate (Kuschminder 2017a), or to engage in circularity (Gemi 2017). We investigate the micro level, notably how individual migrants make sense of their situation, ponder on their options, and take their decisions. We assume that migrants have a bounded rationality, that is, they take their decisions influenced by rational but also emotional cost–benefit considerations in an imperfect information environment and under higher or lower pressure and (un)certainty levels. We consider conditions at origin and destination as the macro level and pay special attention to the policies not only of destination countries but also of the origin country. We analyse the networks, social capital, and specific local context within which each migrant and their household take their decisions as the meso level that mediates between the macro-level conditions and the micro-level processes.

Studying southeastern Europe: case study and research methodology

This book explores the interrelated processes of return, reintegration, remigration, or circulation in the migration system composed by Albania, Italy, and Greece. Our aim is to both cast light on the specific case study and its dynamics – under the pressure of the global and Eurozone financial crisis of the 2010s – but also to explore the micro- and meso-factors and their role in shaping migration trajectories under changing structural conditions (economic crisis, steep rise of unemployment). Our study is based on multi-sited ethnographic fieldwork and two sets of semi-structured interviews with Albanian return migrants conducted between 2014 and 2017.

Albanians are the largest and longer-settled migrant community in Greece and the second-largest migrant group in Italy. Arriving in Greece and Italy without papers as single male workers in the early 1990s and developing later into a family migration, they have integrated into the Greek and Italian societies despite the absence of formal integration policies. Albanians have long struggled to overcome irregularity and had largely managed to do so until the 2009 economic crisis (that hit both countries) which left many among them unemployed. The de-regularization of male wage-earners oftentimes led entire families to lose their legal status. In addition, protracted unemployment of men and a reduction of work/income for women made living in Greece and Italy economically unsustainable for many (Mai and Paladini 2013). This situation of crisis led large numbers of Albanians to return to their country of origin. As recent studies have shown (Maroukis and

Gemi 2013; Mai and Paladini 2013; Gemi 2017) such return patterns included various forms of atypical migration: formal or informal circular mobility, seasonal and on-call employment, transnational economic activities (transport services or petty trade), or remigration back to Italy and Greece or to a third country (e.g. UK or Germany). This background makes of the triptych Albania–Italy–Greece an optimal migration system for exploring the dynamics of return, reintegration, remigration, and circularity in Europe today.

Research methodology

This study builds on two sets of semi-structured interviews with 67 Albanian returnees (from Greece and Italy) of first and second generations, spanning a time cohort of three years: 2014–2017 (Table 1.1; further details can be found in Appendices A–C).

The study is qualitative in nature, based on an ethnographic multi-sited approach. Since the total number of Albanian returnees remains unknown, we opted for purposive sampling and used the snowball method to recruit our informants. The interviewees were selected according to the following criteria: (a) they were over 16 years old; (b) they had stayed for more than one year as a migrant in Greece or Italy; (c) they returned to Albania no earlier than 2010–2011; and (d) they had lived there for at least two months at the time of the interview.

The first set of fieldwork collected information from 31 interviews in Albania with return migrants from Italy (15) and Greece (16) between March and April 2014. The second set of fieldwork draws on

Table 1.1 List of interviews, 2014–2017

Year	Country of reference	Location*	Generation	Total no.
2014	Greece	Tirane/Shkoder/Durres	First generation	16
	Italy	Tirane/Shkoder	First generation	15
2017	Greece	Tirane/Shkoder/Lezhe	First generation	10
			Second generation	10
	Italy	Tirane/Shkoder/Lezhe	First generation	10
			Second generation	6
Total				**67**

Source: authors' compilation

*Location where interviewees live and where interviews were conducted.

20 interviews in Albania with returnees of first generation from Italy (10) and Greece (10) and 16 interviews with young adults of second generation (6 from Italy and 10 from Greece) in February–April 2017. Each time cycle coincides with and reflects specific dynamics, generated mostly by the intensity of the economic crisis and its impact on migrants' livelihood along with political developments at the national and regional levels. For instance, when the first set of interviews were taking place, evidence referred to regular migrants losing legal status and lapsing back into irregularity due to high unemployment rates. During the same period, it was estimated that 130,000 to 140,000 Albanian migrant workers in Greece lost their stay permits because they were unable to secure the required number of social insurance stamps (IKA) in order to renew their documents. In addition, it is estimated that over 180,000 Albanians had returned to Albania in search of better employment prospects there (ACIT 2012). Meanwhile, the second set of interviews focused on patterns of return, reintegration challenges, and mobility dynamics as evidence confirming that return flows have had led to reduction in the stock of Albanians in Greece and Italy (King 2017: 18).

Both sets of interviews took place in three locations: Tirane, Shkodra, and Lezha. The criteria for choosing these locations were based on the evidence from INSTAT and IOM (2014), according to which the largest number of returnees settles in Tirane; Albanians returning from Italy are the majority in two prefectures, Durrës and Shkodër, while Lezhë also attracts a sizeable number of Albanians returning from Italy and Greece. Both sets of interviews were conducted in Albanian and in four cities, namely Tirane, Durres, Shkoder and Lezhe.

The contents of this book

The book is organized into five chapters. Chapter 2 discusses the relevant literature on return, reintegration, remigration, and transnationality/circularity, bringing it together to develop our own analytical framework. We provide operational definitions of migration systems and migration corridors with a view to explaining our broader approach to return, reintegration, and onward migration. We also discuss the notion of migrant agency in light of the recent literature. The chapter then zooms in on both classical theories of return and reintegration (e.g. Bovenkerk, Cerase, Lee) and more recent ones (Cassarino, Kuschminder) with a view to understanding the Albania–Italy–Greece migration system through their lenses. We also consider circularity in both its legal and irregular or informal forms and review the relevant literature that focuses on southeastern Europe and the dynamics of that specific region.

Chapter 3 analyses return, reintegration, remigration, and circular mobility as this is experienced by first-generation Albanians returning from Italy and Albania or Greece and Albania. Chapter 4, on the other hand, focuses on the patterns of return, reintegration, emigration, and circularity of second-generation returnees – notably children born abroad or who moved there at a very young age who returned with their families to Albania as adolescents or young adults. The dynamics analysed in both chapters investigate the relationship between preparedness for return (real and perceived), return and decisions (or concrete plans) for staying, remigrating, or engaging in circular mobility. We consider reintegration as a potential for both onward migration or settlement in the country of origin and look at the decisive factors that eventually lead to leaving or staying. We also look at the relationship between return and engaging in circularity, investigating the importance of structural factors like employment opportunities and migration restrictions (or available options), but also at cultural and social factors like networks in both countries and feelings of belonging to either. In short, we explore the extent to which return and reintegration can breed a transnational living, whether by choice or by necessity. We also pay attention to the gender dimension throughout the study, looking at how gender impacts plans and opportunities for return, remigration, or circularity, and to the urban vs rural divide given that earlier studies suggest different strategies of internal migration or remigration for cities and rural areas.

The final chapter discusses the similarities and differences between the two generations, looking at the impact of both socio-economic factors (skills and qualifications, employment, knowledge of the language) and cultural factors (feelings of belonging, networks at destination or origin). We thus re-elaborate our analytical insights on the dynamic nature of return, reintegration, remigration, and circularity and develop a relevant typology. The chapters are not organized by reference to the specific destination country (Greece or Italy) but rather deal with them as one migration system, identifying the common or different dynamics and mechanisms at play with a view to highlighting the transnational/regional character of these return, remigration, and circulation flows.

References

ACIT (2012) *Study on the Economic Impact of the Greek Crisis in Albania.* Available at: www.usaid.gov/sites/default/files/documents/1863/USAID%20Study%20on%20Greek%20Crisis.pdf [Accessed 8 September 2020].

Bovenkerk, F. (1974) *The Sociology of Return Migration: A Bibliographic Essay.* The Hague: Martinus Nijhoff.

Cassarino, J. P. (2014) A Case for Return Preparedness. In: Battistella, G. (ed.) *Global and Asian Perspectives on International Migration* (Global Migration Issues 4), pp. 153–166. Berlin: Springer.

Cerase, F. (1974) Expectations and Reality: A Case Study of Return Migration from the United States to Southern Italy. *The International Migration Review,* 8 (2), 245–262.

Gemi, E. (2017) Albanian Migration in Greece: Understanding Irregularity in Time of Crisis. *European Journal of Migration and Law,* 19 (1), 12–33.

Gmelch, G. (1980) Return Migration. *Annual Review of Anthropology,* 9, 135–159.

INSTAT and IOM (2014) *Return Migration and Reintegration in Albania 2013.* Tirane: INSTAT/IOM. Available at: www.instat.gov.al/media/2965/return_migrationand_reintegration_in_albania_2013.pdf [Accessed 8 September 2020].

King, R. (2018) Is Migration a Form of Development Aid Given by Poor to Rich Countries? *Journal of Intercultural Studies,* 39 (2), 114–128.

King, R. (2017) *Return Migration and Development: Theoretical Perspectives and Insights from the Albanian Experience.* Keynote lecture to the 2nd Annual Conference of the Western Balkans Migration Network – 'Migration in the Western Balkans: What Do We Know?', Sarajevo, 19–20 May.

Kuschminder, K. (2017a) *Reintegration Strategies: conceptualizing how return migrants Reintegrate.* London: Palgrave.

Kuschminder, K. (2017b) Interrogating the Relationship between Remigration and Sustainable Return. *International Migration,* 55 (6),107–121.

Lee, E. S. (1969) A Theory of Migration. In: Jackson, J. A. (ed.) *Migration.* Cambridge: Cambridge University Press, pp. 282–297.

Loizou, E., Michailidis, A., and Karasavvoglou, A. (2014) Return Migration: Evidence from a Reception Country with a Short Migration History. *European Urban and Regional Studies,* 21 (2), 161–174.

Mai, N. and Paladini, C. (2013) Flexible Circularities: Integration, Return and Socio-Economic Instability within Albanian Migration to Italy. In: Triandafyllidou, A. (ed.) *Circular Migration between Europe and its Neighbourhoods: Choice or Necessity?* Oxford: Oxford University Press, pp. 42–68.

Maroukis, T. and Gemi, E. (2013) Albanian Circular Migration in Greece: Beyond the State? In: Triandafyllidou, A. (ed.) *Circular Migration between Europe and its Neighbourhood: Choice or Necessity?* Oxford: Oxford University Press, pp. 68–90.

Nadler, R., Lang, T. Glorius, B., and Kovács, Z. (2016) Conclusions: Current and Future Perspectives on Return Migration and Regional Development in Europe. In: Nadler, R., Kovács, Z., Glorius, B., and Lang, T. (eds) *Return*

Migration and Regional Development in Europe. Mobility Against the Stream. Basingstoke: Palgrave Macmillan, pp. 291–376.
Thilo, L., Glorius, B., Nadler, R., and Kovács, Z. (2016) Introduction: Mobility Against the Stream? New Concepts, Methodological Approaches and Regional Perspectives on Return Migration in Europe. In: Nadler, R., Kovács, Z., Glorius, B., and Lang, T. (eds) *Return Migration and Regional Development in Europe. Mobility Against the Stream*. Basingstoke: Palgrave Macmillan, pp. 1–22.
Triandafyllidou, A. (2017a). Beyond Irregular Migration Governance. Zooming in on Migrants' Agency. *European Journal of Migration and Law*, 19 (1), 1–11.
Triandafyllidou, A. (2017b) Multicultural Governance in a Mobile World: An Introduction. In: Triandafyllidou, A. (ed.) *Multicultural Governance in a Mobile World*. Edinburgh: Edinburgh University Press, pp. 1–19.
Triandafyllidou, A. (ed.) (2013) *Circular Migration between Europe and its Neighbourhoods: Choice or Necessity?* Oxford: Oxford University Press.
Triandafyllidou, A. and Hatziprokopiou, P. (2013). *Governing Irregular Migration: States, Migrants and Intermediaries at the Age of Globalisation*. ARISTEIA Concept paper, ELIAMEP. Available at: http://irma.eliamep.gr/wp-content/uploads/2013/04/IRMA-Concept-Paper-EN.pdf [Accessed 8 September 2020].

2 Setting the analytical framework
Reconceptualizing return, reintegration, and mobility

Introduction: migration, agency, and migration systems

Migration is a powerful lever of social and economic development and, at the same time, an important concern as it comes with many benefits but also significant challenges and inequalities. Governments of both origin and destination countries are eager to find ways to regulate and govern international migration, which is also testified by the title and objectives of the Global Compact on Safe, Orderly and Regular Migration (United Nations 2018). Oftentimes though both scholarly and policy approaches seeking to understand and regulate the complex drivers of migration, return, and remigration tend to overlook the viewpoint of the migrants (and their households) and the complex socio-economic, political, cultural, and even health-related factors shaping their decisions in an environment that is constantly evolving (Koikkalainen et al. 2019; Syed Zwick 2019). The efforts to engage also with transit and origin countries into migration partnerships and cooperative relations often seem to disregard the interests and concerns of these countries' governments and citizens (Collett and Ahad 2017; Mouthaan 2019; Winters and Izaguirre Mora 2019) as well as the complex dynamics within migration systems (Olumuyiwa et al. 2019) and the links between migration, return, reintegration, and onward migration.

We adopt a complexity approach (Scholten 2020; Verweij and Thompson 2006), investigating migrant decision-making within an intricate and dynamic environment that involves two countries of destination and one country of origin. Our analysis develops through an iterative process, starting with the theoretical insights discussed in this chapter, followed by the analysis of our interview materials in Chapter 3 and Chapter 4, and further refining our analytical framework in the fifth and last chapter of this book.

12 Setting the analytical framework

Our study starts from the premise that the drivers of migration and underlying conditions are themselves evolving; migrants operate in a non-equilibrium environment and develop significant resilience in adapting to changing circumstances, whether at destination or when returning or moving again. Earlier research (Scoones 2004) looking at pastoral systems and their resilience but also at the ways in which critical infrastructure systems, financial markets, or health services react to disease outbreaks (Scoones 2019) points to the need for acknowledging uncertainty and complexity in order to understand how migration systems work.

In recent years there has been increasing attention on migrant decision-making and agency in the middle of contingencies and structural constraints, looking at how migrants take their decisions to migrate. The relevant literature has examined the role of desire, hope, and imagination, biased perception of risk, the type of agency that migrants develop, and the interplay between motivation, opportunity, and ability to migrate with structural constraints – whether social, economic, or political (Koikkalainen and Kyle 2016; Belloni 2016; Bal and Willems 2014; Carling and Schewel 2018; Carling and Collins 2017; Bivand Erdal and Oeppen 2017; Triandafyllidou 2019). There has thus been a shift from the notion of push and pull factors for migration to a more interactive approach of drivers of migration, distinguishing also between the aspiration to migrate and the capacity to do so. This book builds on this scholarly work and adopts a comprehensive approach to the experience of Albanian (return) migrants from Italy and Greece, looking at how they take their decisions to return and then stay in Albania or remigrate within a given context where they have specific pathways available, a desire and a need to migrate, and a certain level of resources that they can mobilize (whether in terms of material resources or networks). We also acknowledge that migrant agency involves degrees of voluntariness and agency or that migrants may feel they are forced to migrate or return. Forced here is not understood in the sense of fleeing persecution or violence (i.e. seeking asylum) but rather as a stringent set of conditions that limit one's choices and push one towards a specific direction. Albanian migration had been defined at its origins in the 1990s as 'economic refugeehood' given the collapse of the Communist regime and of the Albanian economy and state infrastructure and the massive emigration of Albanian citizens throughout the 1990s. We thus feel that it is important to account for the different degrees of voluntariness (see also Ottonelli and Torresi 2013), proactive planning of migration or return, or accounts of feeling obliged by circumstances to return or remigrate as these are subjectively experienced by migrants. We also account for acquiescent vs involuntary immobility (Carling 2002; Schewel 2015) where migrants may feel obliged to stay in Albania because they do not have options for remigrating while they may actually choose to stay (acquiescent immobility) because they do not wish to migrate regardless of their capability to leave (Schewel 2015).

In order to make sense of how migrants make decisions to return, stay, or move from one country to another or indeed to the initial destination, we seek to identify tipping points or critical junctures where the migrant's decision-making is triggered. Crises have been theorized in migration research mostly in relation to humanitarian factors (Martin et al. 2014; Lindley 2014). The 2015–2016 refugee emergency in Europe, however, has given rise to an important critical debate as to who defines, and for whom, what is a crisis (Krzyzanowski et al. 2018), while there has been widespread discussion during the 2010s about the impact of the global financial crisis of 2008–2009 (Ghosh 2013). We acknowledge the complexity and pitfalls of crisis as a concept, and even though the period we study in relation to Albanian return migration is closely linked to the 2008 global financial crisis and the ensuing Eurozone crisis and its impact on Italy and Greece, we opt for a broader operational definition of tipping points or critical junctures that we explore through the interviewees' narratives. Thus, we look for socio-economic drivers that include aspects of the financial crisis, for instance unemployment and reduced income, examining how these interact with each migrant's or household's specific situation.

We investigate how choices for moving or staying (Zickgraf 2018) may be highly gendered and also determined by age and household composition (Gioli and Milan 2018). Recent research (Veronis 2014) has shown that the responsibilities of women in the household varies in different spatial and cultural contexts and shapes their participation (or not) in local or international migration.

In the next section we discuss how we build on insights from the theoretical approaches of migration systems and migration networks and on recent advances on the study of migrant agency in order to construct an analytical framework that brings together these macro, meso, and micro levels helping us understand the dynamics of return, reintegration, and onward migration.

Migration systems, migrant networks, and migrants' agency

This study ultimately focuses on the micro level of migrant agency (see also Triandafyllidou 2017, 2019). In analysing the individual and household level agency of return migrants from Greece and Italy to

Albania, we bring together the macro- and meso-level factors that condition the micro level of individual and household agency.

We conceptualize the macro level as a migration system that brings together the three countries. A migration system is here defined as two or more countries connected to each other by flows and counterflows of people, goods, services, and information (Mabogunje 1970; Faist 1998; de Haas 2009). A migration system involves situations of quasi-organized migratory flows (Mabogunje 1970), which by linking people, families, and communities over space, often result in a 'geographical structuring and clustering of migration flows' (de Haas 2009: 9). Close geographical distance among the countries that make part of a migration system neither precludes nor guarantees sustained relations and migration flows; albeit in the case of Albania, Italy, and Greece, their geographical proximity does facilitate flows, particularly when such flows are not regular, as it reduces transportation and transaction costs.

Migration systems are not established solely by the fact of movement as such, but rather by a 'cumulative causation' effect of past migrations (Massey et al. 1993), as *'settled migrants' presence generates chain migration, evolving into transnational communities which facilitate further migration'* (Doomernik and Kyle 2004: 266). This is certainly a feature of the Albania, Italy, and Greece migration system as we shall illustrate in Chapters 3 and 4. Traditionally, the migration systems' approach viewed migrant settlement as an end-state and static process based on the assumption that once migrants have settled in the country of destination, the migratory flow becomes self-perpetuating since it tends to establish socio-economic structures (see e.g. networks) which are phenomenally able to sustain the process (Castles and Miller 2009; Bakewell et al. 2011). In light of this, it is suggested that it is the migration network theory that provides a better analytical explanation for the emergence of migration systems (Faist 2000; Massey et al. 1993).

Specifically, migration network theory lays strong emphasis on explaining how the past migration experience, the settled migrants, and established ethnic communities in specific countries of destination facilitate the arrival of new migrants (Stark and Wang 2002). In fact, it is commonly known that the social capital embedded within migrant networks in receiving countries lowers the costs and risks of migration movements, and hence increases the likelihood of new migration flows (Bashi 2007). This approach, however, tends to neglect the structural or contextual implications that migration flows have on both the sending and receiving countries' contexts at macro level which is best captured by the migration systems perspective. The initial conditions under which migration once took place may change as a result of external factors such as the economic crisis in both Greece and Italy, the rise in unemployment and underemployment, the decline in remittances to Albania, and the continuously precarious legal status of Albanian migrants in both Greece and Italy.

Thus, bringing together a migration system macro-level perspective and a migrant network meso-level perspective we must not lose sight of their dynamic and evolving nature. Macro factors are not static but are also contextually evolving. A migration system, therefore, can be altered by important changes in the initial socio-economic conditions that shaped it and under which migration unfolded (de Haas 2010). In the case at hand, the global financial crisis and the particularly acute economic crisis in Greece (and to a lesser extent in Italy) reshaped the relevant migration system of Albania, Italy, and Greece.

In addition, the meso level of the transnational, ethnic, and social networks that emerge play an important role in mitigating the effects of the structural changes above and framing the micro level of migrant agency. Last but not least, migrants exercise their agency by developing new strategies for responding to the evolving situation (Gemi 2014: 13). It is important therefore to acknowledge that migration involves changing, often fragmented, trajectories with several 'stop' and 'go' and 'return' moments.

The role of migrant agency is crucial here as a pivotal element that brings together the analysis of the structural factors built into the migration system, the networks that develop, and the contextual changes. Agency implies that the migrant is able to exert a certain degree of control over structural factors and social relations. But more importantly agency here denotes the intentional action of the migrant who seeks to navigate a set of given conditions and opportunity structures as they evolve. Our framework includes the analysis of the macro-level conditions (restrictive migration policies, short permit duration, overall economic crisis) and the meso-level factors (existence of important support networks that can be mobilized), with a view to focusing on the micro level of the migrant and how they develop new strategies and delves into alternative pathways within restricted conditions. Looking at the meso level, we also acknowledge the role of values and culture, notably the emergence of a 'culture of migration' within a particular migration system (Massey et al. 1993: 453). This is often strongly associated with individual socio-economic success, thereby turning migration into a prevailing social norm or a rite of passage for young adults and for entire households.

The proposed framework of macro, meso, and micro level offers several vantage points for studying the return, reintegration, and mobility of Albanian migrants in the context of the Albania, Italy, and Greece migration system. The notion of a migration system points to the importance of looking at both the countries of destination and the country of origin and drawing comparisons among the two destination countries, as well as examining possible multi-directional or onward migration movements, such as from Albania to Greece/Italy and then return to Albania, re-emigration to Greece/Italy, and onward migration to third countries.

The focus on the meso-level factors of networks and values (the culture of migration) allows us also to delve into the inter-generational dimension of these complex migrant trajectories. Within the same household there can be different trajectories for the first- and second-generation migrants and their return, reintegration, and onward migration trajectories. Putting these elements within wider migration system framework allows for factoring in the policies of all three countries and how they dynamically shape the decisions and actions of both first- and second-generation migrants, often in different directions.

The migration systems theory also offers a perspective for analysing the system's decline (de Haas 2010: 30) which may happen if (among other factors) additional legal migration restrictions are imposed that result in increasing costs of migration and the creation of negative social capital for settled migrants. The decline of a migration system does not necessarily imply an overall decline in migration flows but may instead indicate the emergence of new destinations.

The study of the Albania, Italy, and Greece migration system may offer interesting insights as to the dynamics and evolution – coming of age, decline, or rejuvenation – of a migration system. As King (2012) argued, migration systems can be (a) self-feeding through chain migration; (b) self-regulating, deriving from ability to shape its dynamics according to the scale and magnitude of the system's crisis; and (c) self-modifying by shifting migration flows to a different destination when the initial one has been exhausted. In Chapter 5 we explore how the first- and second-generation return, reintegration, and onward migration patterns allow us to gain further insights into the lifecycle of migration systems.

Albanian migration in the context of the southern Europe–western Balkans migration sub-system

Albania, Italy, and Greece form part of the wider EU migration system which is characterized by a high degree of heterogeneity among countries in relation to their experiences and approaches to migration and integration (MEDAM 2017: 5). It is exactly this heterogeneity of migration realities in Europe that give shape to different migration sub-systems including the one under study in this book that we may label as the southeastern Europe–western Balkans migration system, within which Greece, Italy, and Albania form a further sub-unit. European migration sub-systems have emerged in the post-1989 period in line with pre-existing 'privileged' relations between specific origin and destination countries that shared historical cultural and political affinities (Fassmann and Münz 1994) or as is the case for Italy, Greece, and Albania, a history of tense ethnic or territorial relations. Indeed, these inter-country historical linkages formed the context within which specific migration policies emerged, particularly in relation to pre-existing ethnic or cultural ties and the related granting (or not) of preferential migration pathways to certain populations. In fact, these double standard policies – discussed in further detail particularly as regards Greek and Italian co-ethnics from Albania and their preferential pathways to permits, welfare benefits, and ultimately citizenship (Gemi 2016; Triandafyllidou and Kokkali 2010) – have played a crucial role in giving impetus and shaping initial migration patterns, which later tended to develop their own momentum through the self-perpetuating dynamics channelled by migrant networks (de Haas 2007: 35).

Four factors are seen to shape the southern Europe-western Balkans migration sub-system: the shared history of the region; the historical cultural ties among countries in the region and those who joined the EU early on; the pre-existence of migrant networks from Communist times; and (selective) migration policies particularly applied by receiving countries (Kupiszewski et al. 2009: 9). Indeed, despite the relatively closed borders of the Cold War period, emigration was not a new phenomenon for the countries of the western Balkans or southern Europe. Both Italians and Greeks – and likewise the citizens of the former Yugoslavia – migrated to northern and western European countries such as Germany, France, or Belgium in the post-war decades. Albania, however, was an exception as its borders remained hermetically closed during those decades. The fall of the Iron Curtain fundamentally changed the dynamics in the entire region by transforming several southeastern European countries like Albania or Bulgaria nearly 'overnight' into countries of massive emigration, while Greece alongside Italy experienced significant immigration that actually developed in the absence of appropriate migration governance systems. These migration flows took place under a variety of statuses whether as labour migration, asylum-seeking, or simply through irregular channels.

Focusing more specifically on our sub-system of interest – notably Albania, Italy, and Greece – the massive 'exodus' of Albanians starting in the early 1990s and continuing on a massive scale until the end of that decade towards these two neighbouring countries merits some special attention. Albanian migration to Greece and Italy can be categorized into three types: (1) ethnic migration that emerged as a combination of 'voluntary return' to the 'ancient motherland' (the case of Albanians of Greek and Italian decent fleeing to Greece and Italy in the early 1990s) and special benefits deriving from their 'privileged' status (i.e. special pension schemes and access to citizenship) compared to 'other' migrants; (2) trafficking in human beings which is the greatest scourge in the contemporary history of the region (throughout the post-1989 period); and (3) labour migration which has taken several regular or irregular forms (i.e. circular migration mainly involving semi-skilled and unskilled persons) as we shall explain in more detail below, including the newly-emerged category of (economic) 'asylum seekers'.

In the post-1989 period Albanian suffered a significant decline in its resident population due mainly to massive emigration. The country registers one of the world's highest emigration rates, with emigrants accounting for nearly 36 per cent of the total population (INSTAT 2018). According to the Albanian Institute of Statistics, there are over 1,584,137 Albanian citizens living outside the country (INSTAT 2018), with half of those residing in the two countries of interest, notably Greece (23 per cent or 359,994) and Italy (28 per cent or 440,000).

This large-scale migration has also had an important impact on the socio-economic situation in Albania, both by alleviating unemployment pressures and most importantly through the remittances sent back to the country from Albanians abroad (Maroukis and Gemi 2011; Gedeshi and King 2018a). Remittances accounted for 12.3 per cent of the Albanian GDP through the 1990s and 2000s, while they declined in the early 2000s (by 5.8 per cent of GDP) as a result of the global financial crisis and the Eurozone crisis (World Bank 2015). Since then, they have recovered and reached 8.2 per cent of GDP in 2017 (Banka e Shqiperise 2019). According to the Bank of Albania (ibid.), remittances increased during the period 2015–2018, from 597 million euros in 2015 to 670 million euros in 2018. Of those, 34 per cent were from Albanian migrants in Italy and 32 per cent from those in Greece.

The Eurozone crisis of the early 2010s not only led to a drop in remittances from Greece and Italy but also to rampantly rising unemployment among Albanian migrants settled in the two countries

(Maroukis and Gemi 2013; Mai and Paladini 2013; Gemi 2016) and significant return flows towards Albania. It is estimated that 133,544 Albanian emigrants over 18 years of age returned to Albania during the period 2009–2013 alone (INSTAT and IOM 2014). Return flows increased especially after 2009, and the majority of returns occurred in 2012 and 2013 (53.4 per cent) (Ministry of Interior of Albania 2015).

During the last decade, the southern EU-western Balkans migration system entered a transition period. Both Albania and other western Balkan countries have been undergoing two transitions: first, from a region of unstable migration patterns to a region with a relatively stable migration flow; and, second, from a region of emigration to one of transit, circular, and return/remigration flows. The region experienced massive transit flows in 2015–2016 as hundreds of thousands of asylum seekers and migrants transited from Turkey to Greece and Bulgaria, North Macedonia, and through different paths further north and east to Germany and Sweden. Numerous Albanians took advantage of the situation and joined the massive flows seeing an opportunity to move to Germany but their asylum applications were rejected and they were soon returned to Albania (Gemi 2019). Indeed, asylum-seeking had become the only 'regular route' for unskilled and semi-skilled Albanian workers who sought to move north while faced with unemployment or underemployment at home (especially for those returnees from Greece), whereas others engaged into circular routes between Albania and Italy or Albania and Greece (Maroukis and Gemi 2013; Mai and Paladini 2013). Although intended only for tourism, the introduction of a visa-free regime for Albanians entering the Schengen zone (that came into force in January 2011) had a predictable aggravating impact on the informal employment of Albanian migrants who moved to Italy or Greece for short periods of time to work in construction or agriculture.

It is in this socio-economic and geopolitical context of stabilized albeit also mixed migration flows, simultaneous pressures for return and remigration, as well as some transit migration in the southern Europe and western Balkans migration sub-system, that we could come to delve into the macro, meso, and micro factors that shape return, reintegration, and further mobility. The dense historical and socio-economic relations and sustained flows during the post-1989 period, and the overall transformation that this migration sub-system has experienced since the 2010s, offer a particularly suitable case study to apply and also test our analytical framework. In the next section we turn to discuss the particular configurations that return, reintegration, and further mobility take by analysing the macro and meso drivers that affect them. After developing our analytical framework in the next sections of this chapter, in Chapter 2 and Chapter 3 we turn to a closer analysis of the micro level, notably of migrants' agency.

Bringing together return, reintegration, and onward mobility

Return migration can be understood as an inherent feature of migration. In the list of migration laws introduced by Ravenstein back in 1885, the fourth law states that: '*each main current of migration produces a compensating counter-current*' (Ravenstein 1885: 33). In the early theories of migration in the 1970s, return migration was conceptualized as the result of economic crisis. Concomitant changes in the dynamics of migration trajectories took into consideration the key role of the origin country (Bovenkerk 1974: 7). In 1969, Lee developed a theoretical migration model based on a continuum of plus and minus factors in both countries of origin and settlement (the push and pull factors), seeking to explain return migration as a change in the balancing out of the constellation of each set of factors.

In his later work, Bovenkerk (1974: 7) distinguished between three categories relevant to return migration, paving the ground for later research developments on the subject: (a) the shorter the distance of emigration, the higher the incidence of return migration; (b) the longer the emigrants stay away, the less chance there is that they will return; and (c) changes in the economic balance between the place of origin and the place of destination directly affect the volume of return migration. Following from this matrix of push and pull factors, one may come across alternative terminology used to capture the dynamic of return migration such as back migration, counter-current, counter-flow, re-emigration, remigration, return flow, or second-time migration (Bovenkerk 1974: 4). Obviously, these terms are not simply employed to describe a unilinear route back, but rather imply something much more complex than just a journey back to one's 'homeland'. For the sake of clarification, *return migration* is used when emigrants return for the first time to their 'home' country; *re-emigration* when they resettle once again at the same destination after having returned; *second-time emigration* when they emigrate to a new destination after having returned; and *circulation* refers to to and fro movement between two places that includes more than one return (Bovenkerk 1974: 5).

During the last 50 years, several theoretical approaches on return migration have been developed. Relying on the assumption that people make rational decisions to maximize their well-being, the neo-classical economics theory of Harris and Todaro (1970) views migration as an attempt by individuals to maximize their utility by moving to places where they can be more productive. They calculate costs versus benefits of migration, taking into account wage differentials, cost of living, and the costs of moving. In this case, return represents a failure scenario in which there was a miscalculation of the expected benefits from migration in relation to the costs that the migrant incurred (King 2017: 12). Contesting this approach, Simon (1955) spoke of 'approximate' rationality or bounded rationality, in which individuals – because of their limited capacity, incomplete information, and limited time available to process the information – look for satisfactory rather than optimal choices (ibid.: 114).

By applying the new economics of migration theory (Stark 1991, in Lang et al. 2016: 11), the focus is directed to the assumption that migration decisions are made at the household level. It means different members doing different things in different places in order to maximize income and spread risk. Returnees, therefore, can be considered as target-oriented migrants returning once the targeted income goal is reached (Constant and Massey 2002). Return therefore represents a success story of a household project that was completed.

Applying a conflict theory approach, neo-Marxist theorists focus on structural elements that frame migratory decisions, such as the political, economic, demographic, or social conditions in both origin and destination countries (Mabogunje 1970; Gmelch 1980; Kritz and Zlotnik 1992). They adopt an explanatory typology by placing emphasis on whether labour market conditions have changed. This means that economic crisis and declining labour demand at destination countries can trigger return migration, while multiple connections between origin and destination countries can further increase return migration flows. In this case, return reflects the 'rejection' or 'exhaustion' of migrant workers, either due to their declining labour power or because of an overall economic recession (Cassarino 2004; King 2017).

Interestingly, the introduction of a transnationalism approach in Migration Studies brought an important shift in the focus of attention by stressing the significance of transnational social spaces for further mobility decisions (Glick Schiller et al. 1992). Those transnational social spaces that develop in the context of migratory movement constitute an important reference point for the socio-spatial orientation and identity development of migrants (Pries 2008). Thus, return is seen as part of the circulatory system embedded in these transnational social and economic spaces.

Furthermore, social networks and migration systems theory emphasized interconnections between 'home' and 'destination' where cross-border social networks and social capital facilitate return movements. These same networks are also a crucial factor for successful reintegration. Institutionalized networks might also play an important role as they can contribute to overcoming structural challenges that might emerge in the context of return migration (Lang et al. 2016: 11), while they also provide the conditions for the transferability of social capital that migrants acquired while abroad. As Cassarino (2004) put it *'social network theory views returnees as migrants who maintain strong linkages with their former places of settlement in other countries'* (ibid.: 265). It means that successful returnees would have generally expanded their social network due to transnational migration, thus providing them further access to resources as well as positions of power as a result of their expanded social capital.

The role of networks is considered particularly crucial in the context of the individual's resource mobilization and preparedness for return. Cassarino's preparedness theory (Cassarino 2004) goes further by adding two more components, namely willingness and readiness, which are also essential as far as the ability of returnees to reintegrate in the country of origin is concerned. In a way, both preparedness and resource mobilization for return can be supported through social networks in the destination and origin countries.

Interestingly, what seems quite relevant to our case is the approach that views return migration from the perspective of the migrant's agency (Triandafyllidou 2019). It is in this line of reasoning that returnees can be understood as reflexive and responsible individuals who assess risks that they perceive as endangering their opportunities for self-actualization, their social position, and their actual existence. Corroborating this argument, William and Baláž (2012) see migration as a phenomenon that is – by definition – informed by risk. This leads to the assumption that migration is a coping strategy against risk through which individuals show resilience and seek to improve their living and working conditions.

A question that arises in these different theoretical perspectives is whether migration is the end of a cycle or whether it is an intermediate point that may lead either to reintegration at origin or to further migration, whether temporary or long term. Indeed, in this book we conceptualize return as a milestone but not the end of the migratory project.

Some scholars (see for instance Gmelch 1980) have defined return migration as *'the movement of emigrants back to their homelands to resettle*' which implies the '*end of the migration cycle*'. Others however pointed to the importance of remigration and of circular migration, where return is temporary and repeated (Kuschminder 2017: 3–5). Recent literature points to return as another step of a larger migration cycle indicating the multiple attachments that migrants develop during their migratory project (Riiskjaer and Nielsson 2008; Stefannson 2006). Cassarino (2014) views the willingness of individual migrants and their level of readiness and preparedness as conditioning the level of reintegration (ibid.: 163). To this end, willingness and readiness to return might reflect the ability of a person to decide how, when, and why it is time to go back home, which, of course, is not a given as the conditions of return may vary substantially. In other words, not all migrants choose to return on their own initiative, nor do they have the readiness to do so. Such various degrees impact on their propensity to reintegrate back home. It follows from this that the lack of preparedness and readiness for return may lead to further onward migration to a third country or to re-emigration to the initial destination.

Accordingly, reintegration might be defined as the process of adaptation, adjustment, and negotiation in the context of the origin country. More specifically, reintegration is the process through which migrants are able to take part in the social, economic, cultural, and political life of their countries of origin (Cassarino 2014: 163).[1] The process of preparedness is shaped by changing circumstances (e.g. contextual factors in sending and receiving countries) referring as such to macro-level factors as well as to the dynamic of social networks offering opportunities and support to overcome problems at the meso level. However, it should be stressed that the act of return is strongly determined by the micro level, notably the agency and ability of individual migrants and their household members to mobilize material and social resources and to shape their own path.

Considering return as one milestone in the migration project, we are interested in exploring how decisions for onward mobility or remigration are taken – and how such onward mobility (to a third country) or re-emigration (to the initial destination country) relate to reintegration. We use here the term mobility to include (a) onward migration (remigration) to a new destination; (b) when people emigrate once again to the same destination after having returned for the first time (re-emigration); (c) when people engage in circular migration after having returned – a process that can also be seen in the light of transnational mobility. Indeed, returnees continue to maintain their transnational networks, which are highly relevant after their return for economic, social, and emotional reasons.

Having said that, Albanian returnees continue to take advantage of the ties with their former country of residence when they are back in Albania and use them to make a living by engaging in post-return transnationalism (Carling and Bivand Erdal 2014: 4). That is, Albanian returnees maintain connections to Greece and Italy that take form of formal attachment via citizenship or indefinite residence permit or economic transnational activities (seasonal employment or seasonal independent economic activities in the tourism and agriculture sectors, especially in Greece) or transnational families (Gemi 2016). Given the impact of economic crisis on Albanian migrants' livelihoods and 'temporary' return as a result, these forms of connections are usually perceived as safety valves in case of unsuccessful return (Mortensen 2014). Yet transnational ties may be seen as a strategy for an easier reintegration in Albania, as a way to take advantage of the resources (or bridging them) in both Albania and Greece/Italy at the same time (Kopliku 2019: 46).

Straddling the above approaches, return is conceptualized as an episode in the process of transnational transfers whose intentions are shaped by changing circumstances (e.g. personal experiences, contextual factors in sending country) and strongly influenced by transnational life opportunities (Nadler et al. 2016: 361). The factors that shape the degree of permanency or temporariness of return migrants are mostly determined by the patterns of reintegration. A successful social and economic reintegration in the country of origin can discourage a new departure but may also lead to plans for remigration if the returnee is only taking time to gather material resources and build social capital for a new move, whether to a third country or to the previous country of migration (re-emigration). Indeed, it is erroneous to think that reintegration automatically discourages remigration and ignore migrants' agency. Return has, to a great extent, become one step in a complex migration pattern, where the movements covered by the rubric of 'return' in the policy discourse can be extremely heterogeneous and the meaning of return rather ambiguous.

This book supports the hypothesis that in the case of southern EU-western Balkans migration (sub) system (see Albanians in Greece and Italy), return, reintegration, and onward mobility are complex and interconnected processes due to a number of both macro- and meso-level factors. At the macro level we consider the overall economic crisis context of the 2010s and the high levels of unemployment and underemployment in both destination countries under study (Greece and Italy) and in Albania; the geographical proximity of the three countries and the high degree of border porosity because of the possibility to travel without tourism visas; the possession of Greek or Italian citizenship (and of long term stay permits) by an increasing number of both first- and second-generation Albanians living in the two countries; and the lack of reintegration support policies in Albania (see also Maroukis and Gemi 2013). At the meso level we identify the low or non-existent degree of preparedness for return and the lack of willingness to return, the strong social and ethnic networks that Albanian migrants dispose at the two destination countries, at origin, and potentially also in third countries where friends and family are settled. Our focus in Chapters 3 and 4 is on examining how these factors interact with migrants' agency to shape different patterns of return, reintegration, and onward migration. Findings from this study will also engage with recent literature on multiple and multi-directional mobility patterns as observed mainly within the EU among EU citizens (Pries 2016) but also in other migration systems such as Germany–Turkey (Pusch 2013) and Mexico–USA (Pries 2016).

A special note is in order here for what concerns the return, reintegration, and onward mobility patterns of the second generation, notably the children of migrants who came back to their parents' country of origin where they had not lived before. One could say that for this group of young people the decision to return or settle in a country that perhaps is not seen as 'home', as they were not born and raised there, differs from their parents. For second-generation returnees, there may be other motivations compared to issues affecting their parents. For example, a recent study by Haartsen and Thissen (2014) looks at young adults' returns to their rural home region of the Netherlands. Of most interest is their observation that for many of these young migrants a 'return' was not interpreted as such since the perception pertaining to forms of belonging and national identification are essentially different from their parents. This is further corroborated by the studies of Christou (2006) and Christou and King (2010) that emphasize the idea that second-generation Greek American returnees have multiple (national) belongings. This might imply that 'belonging' to a country may no longer be the overarching aspiration and a state of hybrid identity is not perceived as a significant social deficit (King and Christou 2011).

In fact, among the first generation the connotations of 'home' and 'belonging' are more fixed compared to the attachments of their children. Therefore, while we can use the term 'return' for the first generation's resettlement back in their homeland, it is problematic to use the same term for the second generation since they are relocating to a country in which they were not born and raised, and their understanding of 'home' can become blurred (King and Kılınc 2016: 168).

Reflecting on the above, we conceptualize the 'second generation' as composed of those born in Greece and Italy or in Albania to two first-generation immigrant parents and taken to Greece or Italy as very young children. We are interested in investigating the extent to which the second generation's experience of growing up within an Albanian family in Greece or Italy prepares them for the possibility of returning to Albania. What are the circumstances and motivations that lead the second generation to settle to their parents 'homeland? To what degree is this an individual or a whole-family decision? Does return migration result from a lack of integration into Greek and Italian society or experiences of racism and discrimination or both? Against this 'push' factor, what are the 'pull' factors drawing the second generation to Albania? And finally – and perhaps most interesting – what is their experience of (re) integration?

Albanian migration in Greece and Italy: understanding the link between return, reintegration, and mobility

There is considerable literature on the return migration of Albanians from Greece and Italy, but there has been far less investigation of the interconnectedness of return, reintegration, and mobility patterns, particularly in time of crisis. Indeed, no systematic and robust evidence on returns apart from small-scale surveys have been produced so far (King 2017: 8), and even less attention has been paid to the factors influencing the patterns of reintegration and the broader sustainability of the return process (Maroukis and Gemi 2013).

A first stream of returns to Albania from neighbouring countries was noted in the early 2000s, often involving multiple moves back and forth until a migrant decided to settle back in Albania. These returnees tend to be relatively young and of working age. Those returns were mostly identified as a failure of these migrants' project and the impossibility of successfully settling at destination, whether for economic or migration status reasons (Barjaba 2018: 221). Many of these returnees had actually been forced to return because of being caught without appropriate legal status; this stream of returns was also related to deficiencies in the migration policy and practice of the two destination countries and the situation of befallen irregularity in which Albanian migrants found themselves (Triandafyllidou and Ambrosini 2011; Triandafyllidou and Maroukis 2010).

The empirical evidence seemed to suggest a 'migration cycle' involving multiple migration episodes prior to settling, either in the host or the country of origin (Labrianidis and Hatziprokopiou 2006).

Meanwhile, many return episodes happened under different forms, including individual voluntary return, organized voluntary return, and forced return (Maroukis and Gemi 2010). These returns did not generally concern entire households but rather single men. Indeed, despite many hurdles faced at destination, those settled in Greece with their families were unlikely to return because of their children having been assimilated in Greece (or Italy) as well as because of concerns with the unstable economic and political situation in Albania (Gemi 2016). For all those who returned with their families, there was evidence of a positive and strong relation between return migration and business ownership (Kilic et al. 2007; Gedeshi and Gjokuta 2008; Germenji and Milo 2009).

As regards transnational mobility, the study conducted by Vullnetari and King (2009) indicates that these practices of Albanian households were increasing during the 2000s and there was an emergent transnational social space, especially encompassing Greece and Italy. Most permanent return migrants were from urban areas, while circular migrants originated from rural areas and regions closer to Greece (i.e. the central and the mountain regions; Piracha and Vadean 2009). Keeping transnational contacts with the host countries helped returnees develop commercial and economic relationships with the host countries (Gedeshi and Gjokuta 2008) and, in this sense, offered opportunities for back-and-forth movements. Geographic proximity facilitated the possibility of short-term return since the option of seasonal or occasional movements for temporary employment remained open and there was always a possibility for remigration thanks to the relevant networks that returnees maintained in the destination country (Hatziprokopiou and Labrianidis 2005: 12).

In terms of reintegration, forced returnees represented the least reintegrated group, with the highest non-participation rate in employment upon return that made them more oriented towards re-migration (Germenji and Milo 2009). This was corroborated by Labrianidis and Kazazi (2006), who pointed out that neither migration nor return was 'permanent' in character. As to the question reintegration patterns and whether return-migration reinforces internal migration, the study of Labrianidis and Kazazi (ibid.) found out that once returned, returnees first settle in the place of origin to build or restore the house, start a new business, and become familiar with Albanian conditions and reality. The second step is internal migration towards the more developed urban areas in search for more job and business opportunities, as well as a better quality of life (ibid.: 72).

Towards the end of the 2000s, as the socio-economic integration of Albanians in both countries started to be institutionalized and finally deepened, the rhythms of forced return started to decrease. After years of being subject to a very particular regime of semi-regularity, the number of long-term residents and naturalized Greek and Italian citizens rose significantly. A comment is in order here regarding the return 'preparedness' of Albanian migrants (Cassarino 2004), which is also shaped by their integration on questions linked to the integration into the host country (Paladini 2014). As far as the integration patterns influence and potentially shape the return dynamics, the term *differential inclusion* is employed to show how migrants are integrated in some sections of society, mainly in the labour market, but denied access to others, like citizenship and political participation in both countries (Mai and Schwandner-Sievers 2003). In Greece, the integration trajectory of Albanians was for a long time that of *partial integration*, which comes as a result of the *differential exclusion* policies (Gemi 2019). For Italy, the term *subordinate integration* is employed to best describe the approach towards migrants' integration (Gropas and Triandafyllidou 2014: 27). Although Greece and Italy differ in size, political organization, economic structure, and national identity definition, their migration policies in the 1990s and 2000s developed along similar directions. These similarities could be attributed to their geographical position in southern Europe, their lack of previous immigration experience, and their large informal economies that have provided for 'informal' employment opportunities for immigrants. In both countries, immigration laws were reactive rather than proactive, seeking to mitigate or channel the impact of migration processes that were already under way without a clear long-term strategy. Naturalization and integration policies were particularly stringent, while long-term residence permits were hard to obtain.

In response to this uncertain and exclusionary context, Albanian migrants adopted a strategy characterized as 'mimesis' (Paladini 2014: 112) or in more politically correct terms *assimilation* (through mimesis). In a way, Albanians persistently sought to blur into the Greek and Italian social fabric, making themselves as 'invisible' as possible by changing their names (as happened in Greece) and religious affiliation (converting at least nominally to Orthodoxy or Catholicism). The term *asymmetric assimilation* adopted by King and Mai (2008: 117) emphasizes exactly the paradox of a community which was at the same time the most stigmatized and the most integrated and similar to the population of the two host countries (Paladini 2014: 112).

It was 2008–2009 that marked a significant increase in migrants returning to Albania (Barjaba 2018: 222). Albanians had long struggled to overcome irregularity and had largely managed to do so, were it not for the 2008 economic crisis that hit both Italy and Greece, leaving many among them unemployed. The de-regularization of male wage-earners oftentimes – those working in the construction sector in particular – led entire families to lose their legal status. Protracted unemployment of men and a reduction of work/income for women made living in Greece and Italy economically unsustainable for many. The transition in which Albanians found themselves reversed, in a way, the process of integration. Since their socio-economic relations and stay had to be re-evaluated, they were found under pressure to re-establish or strengthen ties to their networks in Albania or elsewhere because of the need to face the consequences of the crisis (Gemi 2016: 36). According to the study carried out by the International Organization for Migration (IOM) in Albania in 2013, the majority of returns were voluntary and concerned Albanian migrants who were previously in Greece (70.8 per cent) and Italy (23.7 per cent).

Despite this trend, in the 2010s context, return to Albania did not seem to signal the end of the migration project *per se* and was not stigmatized as failure, as happened in earlier decades. It was rather a strategic move by skilled migrants and entire families who saw this as an attempt to establish themselves again in Albania while leaving open the option of re-emigration at destination (Barjaba 2018). Indeed, the impact of the economic recession, along with the liberalization in 2011 of the entry visa for Albanian citizens to enter the EU for periods of up to 90 days, gave a new dynamic to the mobility patterns of Albanian migration in the region. The circular movements for seasonal, often informal, employment in specific sectors of the economy (e.g. agriculture and tourism) took place in the context of such temporary visits where stay was legal (as per the visa liberalization regime) but work was informal (as such visits do not authorize employment) (Gemi 2016).

During the early 2010s, Albanians in both Greece and Italy considered heading back to Albania or moving towards other industrial countries of western Europe with the aim of finding employment opportunities there (Triandafyllidou 2013; Gemi 2016).This is also confirmed by the fact that the number of Albanian citizens who applied for asylum in EU Member States – 11,040 in 2013 and 12,295 in 2014, with this number growing further in 2014–2017. During 2015, there was a surge of 'economic asylum seekers' who left Albania, heading largely to Germany, the Netherlands, and other western European countries (Barjaba 2018: 220). In total, 53,805 Albanians applied for asylum in Germany in 2015 (Eurostat 2016), pushing Albania into the top four countries of origin of asylum seekers in the

EU that year. These 'asylum seekers', particularly those directed to Germany, were encouraged by signals that the German government was revisiting its migration policies to attract new foreign labour (Barjaba 2018: 220). During these years, the main causes of emigration for Albanian citizens were still of economic nature, among which unemployment and poverty, with 12.5 per cent of the population living below the poverty line (INSTAT 2016) even though the Albanian economy had shown positive (albeit low) rates of growth in 2013–2015 (World Bank 2016).

With a view to elaborating on the new dynamics of return migration, Gedeshi and Xhaferaj (2016) distinguished between two groups of returnees. The first is composed of economic migrants whose return intensity is believed to decrease after 2014. The second is composed of failed asylum seekers who applied mostly between 2014 and 2015, and whose return rose in 2015 and 2016. These findings are confirmed by the latest report published by Albanian government on the migration profile of the returnees (Republic of Albania 2017: 22). Particularly as regards the rejected asylum seekers of 2015–2016, these are in their vast majority men – 94 per cent in 2015 and 85 per cent in 2016 – which probably suggests that those who joined the Balkan path of asylum seekers and migrants were single men trying to emigrate to Germany or other western and northern European countries. Interestingly, 67 per cent of the registered returnees declared that they returned permanently, while 33 per cent considered their return as temporary (ibid.: 25). In interpreting this willingness to remigrate, it is important to consider that the increased returns, the decrease in remittances, and the still-fragile recovery in Greece and Italy had negative mirror effects on the Albanian economy thus fuelling the ranks of those considering remigrating (Hackaj et al. 2016: 7; Kerpaci and Kuka 2015). Corroborating this, Gedeshi and King (2018b) conclude that returnees who have not achieved their migration goals intend to realize them by re-emigrating (ibid.: 72), with 54 per cent of returnees from Italy and around 40 per cent from Greece intending to re-emigrate to the destination countries; the rest of the returnees prefer other destination countries such as Germany, the USA, and the UK. According to the authors, the very high desire to remigrate shows that the level of income and work conditions are not satisfying enough for staying in Albania (ibid.: 73).

In order to address the reintegration challenges of returnees, Gedeshi and Xhaferaj (2016) classify them in five groups: (i) unemployed; (ii) employed; (iii) self-employed; (iv) small and medium investors; and (v) students (ibid.: 20). Their study argues that the most vulnerable group are unemployed returnees with an immediate need for economic assistance and integration of children in schools. The second group is of higher professional level and social capital, which has helped them in finding employment in Albania. The self-employed are in need rather of financial and technical assistance to support their business plans in Albania. Entrepreneurs are characterized by a higher level of human, financial, and social capital but in need of more business consulting and services in education and care. The last group, the returned students, require equal access to and participation in the economic, academic, and political life of the country (ibid.: 26).

Cena (2017), on the other hand, addresses the experiences of (re)settlement and belonging for Albanian return migrants and their children from Greece during the early to mid-2010s. The findings highlight the conditions upon which the return occurred (i.e. unwillingly and without readiness or preparedness), which influence the ability of returnees to reintegrate, particularly with respect to employment and school experiences (ibid.: 210).

Relying on large-scale quantitative data, García-Pereiro and Biscione (2016) in their study of returnees' profiles, suggest that size and intensity of transnational activities are among the most important determinants in shaping the return decisions of Albanian migrants (ibid.: 150). In the same vein, Paladini (2014) distinguishes new forms of transnational space whereby many migrant families preferred to separate, with one parent and the children staying at destination while the other parent seeks employment or business opportunities back in Albania or develops transnational economic activities between the two countries. These strategies involved circular movements between Albania and Italy for both personal reasons and to forge business connections between the two sides of the Adriatic (ibid.: 109).

In conclusion, the patterns of Albanian return migration from Italy and Greece have significantly shifted during the last three decades. While in the 1990s and 2000s returns were largely forced and signified the failure of the migration project, in the 2010s the patterns are much more complex and dynamic. The 2010s have been characterized by increased mobility driven by important macro-level factors: the economic crisis in Italy and Greece, the still-weak economic growth and significant unemployment in Albania, the weak reintegration policies in Albania, and the opportunity to join the Balkan flow and seek asylum in Germany or elsewhere in western Europe. Meso factors however have been crucial in shaping the different strategies of return, reintegration, and onward mobility (whether circular mobility, transnational mobility, re-emigration, or remigration to a third country). These include the existence of important transnational networks in the three countries (Albania, Italy, and Greece), the role of migrant smugglers in encouraging them to try the asylum-seeking path, and the reintegration networks at home. While recent research has shed light on the causes and consequences of return to Albania, we feel there is still a research gap in piecing together the puzzle – notably return, reintegration, circular mobility, transnational mobility, and migration to a third country.

Concluding remarks

The aim of this chapter has been to develop our analytical and conceptual framework for studying return, reintegration, and onward mobility in general and with special reference to the Albania, Italy, and Greece migration system. We have argued that the migration system theoretical framework offers the appropriate tools for factoring in the different macro, meso, and micro elements conditioning Albanians' mobility between these countries during the last decade. After having situated the sub-system formed by these three countries within the larger European framework and the post-1989 period, this chapter analysed the evolution of Albanian return migration in the last three decades and the macro and meso factors that have driven return, remigration, and onward mobility. In the following chapters we analyse the mobility patterns of first-generation returnees (Chapter 3) and those of the second generation (Chapter 4).

Note

1 Social aspects would include participation in organizations, relationships, and acceptance with family and friends (such as respect within the household), access to information sources, and societal acceptance. Cultural aspects would include participating in religious or cultural events, and participation in the norms and values of the society. Economic reintegration refers to the occupational and employment status of the returnee and their ability to afford a certain standard of living. It also includes entrepreneurial activities and local investments. Political reintegration refers to participation in the political process of the country.

References

Bakewell, O., de Haas, H., and Kubal, A. (2011) *Migration Systems, Pioneers and the Role of Agency*. IMI Working Paper Series, 48. Oxford: University of Oxford. Available at: www.imi.ox.ac.uk/pdfs/wp/wp-48-11.pdf [Accessed 8 September 2020].

Bal, E. and Willems, R. (2014) Introduction: Aspiring Migrants, Local Crises and the Imagination of Futures 'Away from Home'. *Identities* 21 (3), 249–258.

Banka e Shqiperise (2019) Nje veshtrim mbi remitancata [An Overview of Remittances]. Available at: www.bankofalbania.org/rc/doc/Fletepalosje_ Remitancat_Shqip_2019_14709.pdf [Accessed 8 September 2020].

Barjaba, K. (2018) Failure of 'Myth of Homeland': Delay of Return Migration to Albania. *Itinerari di ricerca storica*, XXXI, 2.

Bashi, V. F. (2007) *Survival of the Knitted: Immigrant Social Networks in a Stratified World*. Stanford, CA: Stanford University Press.

Belloni, M. (2016) Refugees as Gamblers: Eritreans Seeking to Migrate through Italy. *Journal of Immigrant & Refugee Studies*, 14 (1), 104–119.

Bivand Erdal, M. and Oeppen, C. (2017) Forced to Leave? The Discursive and Analytical Significance of Describing Migration as Forced and Voluntary. *Journal of Ethnic and Migration Studies*, 44 (6), 981–998.

Bovenkerk, F. (1974) *The Sociology of Return Migration: A Bibliographic Essay*. The Hague: Martinus Nijhoff.

Carling, J. (2002) Migration in the Age of Involuntary Immobility: Theoretical Reflections and Cape Verdean Experiences. *Journal of Ethnic and Migration Studies*, 28 (1), 5–42.

Carling, J. and Bivand Erdal, M. (2014) Return Migration and Transnationalism: How Are the Two Connected? *International Migration* 52 (6), 2–12.

Carling, J. and Collins, F. (2017) Aspiration, Desire and Drivers of Migration. *Journal of Ethnic and Migration Studies*, 44 (6), 909–926.

Carling, J. and Schewel, K. (2018) Revisiting Aspiration and Ability in International migration. *Journal of Ethnic and Migration Studies*, 44 (6), 945–963.

Cassarino, J. P. (2004) Theorising Return Migration: The Conceptual Approach to Return Migrants Revisited. *International Journal on Multicultural Societies* 6 (2), 253–279.

Cassarino, J. P. (ed.) (2014) *Reintegration and Development. CRIS Project Analytical Study*. Florence: European University Institute. Available at: www.jeanpierrecassarino.com/wp-content/uploads/2014/03/Reintegration-and-Development-CRIS.pdf [Accessed 8 September 2020].

Castles, S. and Miller, M. (2009). *The Age of Migration: International Population Movements in the Modern World*. Basingstoke: Palgrave Macmillan.

Cena, E. (2017) Return Migration during the Economic Crisis: Experiences of Albanian Return Migrants and Their Children in the Quest to Belong. PhD thesis, Edge Hill University. Available at: https://research.edgehill.ac.uk/files/20511300/Cena_Elida_Thesis_PhD_2017_Final_2017.11.16..pdf [Accessed 8 September 2020].

Christou, A. (2006) *Narratives of Place, Culture and Identity: Second-generation Greek-Americans Return 'Home'*. Amsterdam: Amsterdam University Press.

Christou, A. and King, R. (2010) Imagining 'Home': Diasporic Landscapes of the Greek-German Second Generation. *Geoforum*, 41 (4), 638–646.

Collett, E. and Ahad, A. (2017) *EU Migration Partnerships: A Work in Progress*. Brussels: Migration Policy Institute Europe. Available at: www.migrationpolicy.org/research/eu-migration-partnerships-work-progress [Accessed 8 September 2020].

34 Setting the analytical framework

Constant, A. and Massey, D. (2002) Return Migration by German Guestworkers: Neoclassical versus New Economic Theories. *International Migration* 40 (4), 5–38.

de Haas, H. (2007) *North African Migration Systems: Evolution, Transformations and Development Linkages.* IMI Working Paper 6. Oxford: International Migration Institute, University of Oxford.

de Haas, H. (2010) The Internal Dynamics of Migration Processes: A Theoretical Inquiry. *Journal of Ethnic and Migration Studies* 36, 1587–1617.

de Haas, H. (2009) *Mobility and Human Development.* Nairobi: UNDP. Available at: http://hdr.undp.org/sites/default/files/hdrp_2009_01_rev.pdf [Accessed 8 September 2020].

Doomernik, J. and Kyle, D. (2004) Introduction. *Journal of International Migration and Integration,* 5, 265–272.

Eurostat (2016) Asylum Applicants in the EU. Available at: https://ec.europa.eu/eurostat/news/themes-in-the-spotlight/asylum2016 [Accessed 8 September 2020].

Faist, T. (1998) Transnational Social Spaces out of International Migration: Evolution, Significance and Future Prospects. *Archives Européennes de Sociologie* 39 (2), 213–247.

Faist, T. (2000) *The Volume and Dynamics of International Migration and Transnational Social Spaces.* Oxford: Oxford University Press.

Fassmann, H. and Münz, R. (1994) Austria: A Country of Immigration and Emigration. In: Fassmann, H. and Münz, R. (eds) *European Migration in the Late Twentieth Century. Historical Patterns, Actual Trends, and Social Implications.* Cheltenham: Edward Elgar Publishing, pp. 149–168.

García-Pereiro, T. and Biscione, A. (2016) Return Migration in Albania: the profiles of returnees. *Rivista Italiana di Economia Demografia e Statistica,* LXX (2). Available at: www.sieds.it/listing/RePEc/journl/2016LXX_N2_RIEDS_141-152_Garc%EDa-Pereiro_Biscione.pdf [Accessed 8 September 2020].

Gedeshi, I. and Gjokuta, E. (2008) *Introducing a Migrant City: Tirana.* Tirana: British Council in Albania.

Gedeshi, I. and King, R. (2018a). *Research Study on Brain Gain: Reversing Brain Drain with Albanian Scientific Diaspora.* Tirana: UNDP.

Gedeshi, I. and King, R. (2018b) *New Trends in Potential Migration from Albania.* Tirana: Friedrich-Ebert-Stiftung. Available at: http://library.fes.de/pdf-files/bueros/albanien/15272.pdf [Accessed 8 September 2020].

Gedeshi, I. and Xhaferaj, E. (2016) *Social and Economic Profile of the Return Migrants in Albania.* Tirana: International Organization for Migration.

Gemi, E. (2014) Transnational Practices of Albanian Families during the Greek Crisis: Unemployment, De-regularization and Return. *International Review of Sociology,* 24 (3), 406–421.

Gemi, E. (2016) Integration and Transnational Mobility in Time of Crisis: The Case of Albanians in Greece and Italy. *Studi Emigrazione,* LIII (202), 237–255.

Gemi, E. (2019) *Integration and Transnationalism in a Comparative Perspective: The Case of Albanian Immigrants in Vienna and Athens.* Vienna: Verlag der Österreichischen Akademie der Wissenschaften.

Germenji, E. and Milo, L. (2009) Return and Labour Status at Home: Evidence from Returnees in Albania. *Southeast European and Black Sea Studies*, 9 (4), 497–517.

Ghosh, B. (2013) *The Global Economic Crisis and the Future of Migration: Issues and Prospects. What will Migration Look Like in 2045?* Basingstoke: Palgrave Macmillan.

Gioli, G. and Milan, A. (2018) Gender, Migration and (Global) Environmental Change. In: McLeman, R. and Gemenne, F. (eds) *Routledge Handbook of Environmental Displacement and Migration*. London: Routledge, pp. 135–149.

Glick Schiller, N., Basch, N., and Blanc-Szanton, C. (1992) Transnationalism: A New Analytic Framework for Understanding Migration. *Annals of The New York Academy of Science*, 645, 1–24.

Gmelch, G. (1980) Return Migration. *Annual Review of Anthropology*, 9, 135–159.

Gropas, R. and Triandafyllidou, A. (2014) *Integration, Transnational Mobility and Human, Social and Economic Capital*. Concept Paper for the ITHACA Project. Available at: https://cadmus.eui.eu/handle/1814/31200 [Accessed 20 December 2020]

Haartsen, T. and Thissen, F. (2014) The Success-Failure Dichotomy Revisited: Young Adults' Motives to Return to Their Rural Home Region. *Children's Geographies*, 12 (1), 87–101.

Hackaj, A., Shehaj, E., and Zeneli, N. (2016) *Comprehending Albanian Migration to Germany in the Period 2014–2016*. Working Paper 'Berlin Process Series' 2/2016. Tirana: Cooperation and Development Institute.

Harris, J. R. and Todaro, M. P. (1970) Migration, Unemployment and Development: A Two-Sector Analysis. *The American Economic Review*, 60 (1), 126–142.

Hatziprokopiou, P. and Labrianidis, L. (2005) Albanian Return Migration: Migrants Tend to Return to Their Country of Origin after All. In: King, R., Mai, N., and Schwandner-Sievers, S. (eds) *The New Albanian Migration*. Brighton: Sussex Academic Press, pp. 93–117.

INSTAT (2016) Shqipëria në Shifra, 2016 [Albania in Numbers]. Available at: www.instat.gov.al/al/publikime/librat/2017/shqip%C3%ABria-n%C3%AB-shifra-2016/ [Accessed 8 September 2020].

INSTAT (2018) Diaspora e Shqipërisë në shifra. Available at: www.instat.gov.al/al/publikime/librat/2018/diaspora-e-shqip%C3%ABris%C3%AB-n%C3%AB-shifra-2018/ [Accessed 8 September 2020].

INSTAT and IOM (2014) *Return Migration and Reintegration in Albania 2013*. Tirana: INSTAT/IOM. Available at: www.instat.gov.al/media/2965/return_migration_and_reintegration_in_albania_2013_.pdf [Accessed 8 September 2020].

Kerpaci, K. and Kuka, M. (2015) 'Feeling Like a Migrant Even in My Homeland': Living Experiences of Albanian Return Migrants from Greece. In: *Proceedings of the 10th International Congress of the Hellenic Geographical Society, Special Session 1 (22–24 October 2014, Thessaloniki, Greece)*, pp. 1153–1161. Hellenic Geographical Society.

Kilic, T., Carletto, G., Davis, B., and Zezza, A. (2007) *Investing Back Home: Return Migration and Business Ownership in Albania*. Policy Research Working Paper Series. Washington, DC: World Bank.

King, R. (2012) *Theories and Typologies of Migration: An Overview and a Primer*. Willy Brandt Series of Working Papers in International Migration and Ethnic Relations 3/12. Malmö: Malmö University.

King, R. (2017) *Return Migration and Development: Theoretical Perspectives and Insights from the Albanian Experience*. Keynote lecture to the 2nd Annual Conference of the Western Balkans Migration Network – 'Migration in the Western Balkans: What Do We Know?', Sarajevo, 19–20 May.

King, R. and Christou, A. (2011) Of Counter-diaspora and Reverse Transnationalism: Return Mobilities to and from the Ancestral Homeland. *Mobilities*, 6 (4), 451–466.

King, R. and Kılınc, N. (2016) The Counter-Diasporic Migration of Turkish-Germans to Turkey: Gendered Narratives of Home and Belonging. In: Nadler, R., Kovács, Z., Glorius, B., and Lang, T. (eds) *Return Migration and Regional Development in Europe: New Geographies of Europe*. London: Palgrave Macmillan.

King, R. and Mai, N. (2008) *Out of Albania: From Crisis Migration to Social Inclusion in Italy*. Oxford: Berghahn.

Koikkalainen, S. and Kyle, D. (2016) Imagining Mobility: The Prospective Cognition Question in Migration Research. *Journal of Ethnic and Migration Studies*, 42 (5), 759–776.

Koikkalainen, S., Kyle, D., and Nykanene, T. (2019) Imagination, Hope and the Migrant Journey: Iraqi Asylum Seekers Looking for a Future in Europe. *International Migration*, 58 (4), 54–68.

Kopliku, B. (2019) Re-adjustment in the Home Country – the Effects of Return Migration and Transnationalism. *RSC Research in Social Change*, 11 (1), 42–61.

Krzyzanowski, M., Triandafyllidou, A., and Wodak, R. (2018) The Mediatization and the Politicization of the 'Refugee Crisis' in Europe. *Journal of Immigrant and Refugee Studies*, 16 (1–2), 1–14.

Kupiszewski, M., Kicinger, A., Kupiszewska, D., and Flinterman, F. H. (2009) *Labour Migration Patterns, Policies and Migration Propensity in the Western Balkans*. Available at: https://publications.iom.int/system/files/pdf/labour_migration_patterns_western_balkans.pdf [Accessed 8 September 2020].

Kuschminder, K. (2017) Interrogating the Relationship between Remigration and Sustainable Return. *International Migration*, 55 (6), 107–121.

Kritz, M. M. and Zlotnik, H. (1992) Global Interactions: Migration Systems, Processes, and Policies. In: Kritz, M. M., Lim, L. L., and Zlotnik, H. (eds) *International Migration Systems: A Global Approach*. Oxford: Clarendon Press, pp. 1–16.

Labrianidis, L. and Hatziprokopiou, P. (2006) The Albanian Migration Cycle: Migrants Tend to Return to Their Country of Origin after All. In: King, R., Mai, N., and Schwandner-Sievers S. (eds) *The New Albanian Migration*. Brighton: Sussex Academic Press, pp. 93–117.

Labrianidis, L. and Kazazi, B. (2006) Albanian Return-Migrants from Greece and Italy: Their Impact upon Spatial Disparities within Albania. *European Urban and Regional Studies*, 13 (1), 59–74.

Lang, T., Glorius, B., Nadler, R., and Kovács, Z. (2016) Introduction: Mobility Against the Stream? New Concepts, Methodological Approaches and Regional Perspectives on Return Migration in Europe. In: Nadler, R., Kovács, Z., Glorius, B., and Lang, T. (eds) *Return Migration and Regional Development in Europe: Mobility Against the Stream*. Basingstoke: Palgrave Macmillan, pp. 1–22.

Lee, E. S. (1969) A Theory of Migration. In: Jackson, J. A. (ed.) *Migration*. Cambridge: Cambridge University Press, pp. 282–297.

Lindley, A. (ed.) (2014) *Crisis and Migration: Critical Perspectives*. London: Routledge.

Mabogunje, A. (1970) Systems Approach to a Theory of Rural-Urban Migration. *Geographical Analysis*, 2 (1), 1–18.

Mai, N. and Paladini, C. (2013) Flexible Circularities: Integration, Return and Socio-Economic Instability within the Albanian Migration to Italy. In: Triandafyllidou, A. (ed.) *Circular Migration Between Europe and its Neighbourhood*. Oxford: Oxford University Press, pp. 42–68.

Mai, N. and Schwandner-Sievers, S. (2003) Albanian Migration and New Transnationalisms. *Journal of Ethnic and Migration Studies*, 29 (6), 939–948.

Maroukis, T. and Gemi, E. (2010) *Circular Migration between Albanian and Greece*. Background report, Metoikos Project. Available at: https://core.ac.uk/download/pdf/45680147.pdf [Accessed 8 September 2020].

Maroukis, T. and Gemi, E. (2011) *Circular Migration between Greece and Albania: A Case Study*. Florence: European University Institute.

Maroukis, T. and Gemi, E. (2013) Circular Migration between Greece and Albania: Beyond the State? In: Triandafyllidou A. (ed.) *Circular Migration between Europe and its Neighbourhood: Choice or Necessity*. Oxford: Oxford University Press, pp. 68–89.

Martin, S., Weerasinghe, S., and Taylor, A. (eds) (2014) *Humanitarian Crises and Migration: Causes, Consequences and Responses*. New York: Routledge.

Massey, D. S., Arango, J., Hugo, G., Kouaouci, A., Pellegrino, A., and Taylor, E. J. (1993) Theories of International Migration: A Review and Appraisal. *Population and Development Review* 19 (3), 431–466.

MEDAM (ed.) (2017) *Sharing Responsibility for Refugees and Expanding Legal Immigration*. Assessment Report on Asylum and Migration Policies in Europe. Kiel: Kiel Institute for the World Economy.

Ministry of Interior of Albania (2015) Albania: Extended Migration Profile: 2012–2014. Available at: https://albania.iom.int/sites/default/files/publication/12.%20Albania%20-%20Extended%20Migration%20Profile%202012-2014.pdf [Accessed 8 September 2020].

Mortensen, E. B. (2014) Not Just a Personal Decision. *African Diaspora*, 7 (1), 15–37.

Mouthaan, M. (2019) Unpacking Domestic Preferences in the Policy-'Receiving' State: The EU's Migration Cooperation with Senegal and Ghana. *Comparative Migration Studies*, 7 (35), 7–37.

Nadler, R., Lang, T., Glorius, B., and Kovács, Z. (2016) Conclusions: Current and Future Perspectives on Return Migration and Regional Development in Europe. In: Nadler, R., Kovács, Z., Glorius, B., and Lang, T. (eds) *Return Migration and Regional Development in Europe. Mobility Against the Stream*. Basingstoke: Palgrave Macmillan, pp. 291–376.

Olumuyiwa, O. A., Akanle, O., Falase, O. S., and Oluwatoyin, O. M. (2019) Migration and Environmental Crises in Africa. In: Menjívar, C., Ruiz, M., and Ness, I. (eds) *The Oxford Handbook of Migration Crises*. London: Oxford University Press, pp. 1–10.

Ottonelli, V. and Torresi, T. (2013) When is Migration Voluntary? *International Migration Review*, 47 (4), 783–813.

Paladini, C. (2014) Circular Migration and New Forms of Citizenship. The Albanian Community's Redefinition of Social Inclusion Patterns. *European Journal of Research on Education*, 2 (6), 109–115.

Piracha, M. and Vadean, F. (2009) *Return Migration and Occupational Choice*. Bonn: IZA.

Pries, L. (2008) Transnational Societal Spaces: Which Units of Analysis, Reference, and Measurement? In: Pries, L. (ed.) *Rethinking Transnationalism. The Meso-link of organisations*. London: Routledge, pp. 1–20.

Pries, L. (2016) Circular Migration as (New) Strategy in Migration Policy? Lessons from Historical and Sociological Migration Research. In: Nadler, R., Kovács, Z., Glorius, B., and Lang, T. (eds) *Return Migration and Regional Development in Europe: Mobility against the Stream*. Basingstoke: Palgrave Macmillan, pp. 25–54.

Pusch, B. (2013) *Mirror, Mirror on the Wall, Who Is the Migrant of Us All?* Presentation at International Conference on 'Perceptions of International Migrants in Turkey', Bilgi University, Istanbul, 12 April.

Ravenstein, E. G. (1885) The Laws of Migration. *Journal of the Statistical Society of London*, 48 (2), 167–235.

Republic of Albania (2017) Albania – Migration Profile 2016. Available at: www.mb.gov.al/files/documents_files/Profili_i_Migracionit_2016_(Eng).pdf [Accessed 8 September 2020].

Riiskjaer, M. H. B. and Nielsson, T. (2008) *Circular Repatriation: The Unsuccessful Return and Reintegration of Iraqis with Refugee Status in Denmark*. UNHCR research paper no. 165. Available at: www.refworld.org/docid/4c23256d0.html [Accessed 8 September 2020].

Schewel, K. (2015) *Understanding the Aspiration to Stay: A Case Study of Young Adults in Senegal*. COMPAS Working Paper 107. Available at: www.migrationinstitute.org/publications/wp-107-15 [Accessed 8 September 2020].

Scholten, P. (2020) Mainstreaming versus Alienation: Conceptualizing the Role of Complexity in Migration and Diversity Policy Making. *JEMS Journal of Ethnic and Migration Studies*, 46 (1), 108–126.

Scoones, I. (2004) Climate Change and the Challenge of Non-equilibrium Thinking. *IDS Bulletin* 35 (3), 114–119.
Scoones, I. (2019) *What Is Uncertainty and Why Does it Matter?* STEPS Working Paper 2019/01. Brighton: Institute of Development Studies.
Simon, H. A. (1955) A Behavioral Model of Rational Choice. *The Quarterly Journal of Economics* 69, 99–118.
Stark, O. (1991) *The Migration of Labour.* Oxford: Blackwell.
Stark, O. and Wang, Y. Q. (2002) Migration Dynamics. *Economics Letters*, 76.
Stefannson, A. (2006) Homes in the Making: Property Restitution, Refugee Return, and Senses of Belonging in a Post-war Bosnian Town. *International Migration*, 44 (3), 115–139.
Syed Zwick, H. (2019) Narrative Analysis of Syrians, South Sudanese and Libyans Transiting in Egypt: A MOA Approach. MPRA Paper No. 93041. Available at: https://mpra.ub.uni-muenchen.de/93041/1/MPRA_paper_93041.pdf [Accessed 20 December 2020].
Triandafyllidou, A. (2013). Irregular Migration and Domestic Work in Europe: Who Cares? In: Triandafyllidou, A. (ed.) *Irregular Migration and Domestic Work in Europe: Who Cares?* Farnham: Ashgate, pp. 1–15.
Triandafyllidou, A. (2017) Beyond Irregular Migration Governance. Zooming in on Migrants' Agency. *European Journal of Migration and Law*, 19 (1), 1–11.
Triandafyllidou, A. (2019) The Migration Archipelago: Social Navigation and Migrant Agency. *International Migration*, 57 (1), 5–19.
Triandafyllidou, A. and Ambrosini, M. (2011) Irregular Immigration Control in Italy and Greece: Strong Fencing and Weak Gate-keeping Serving the Labour Market. *European Journal of Migration and Law*, 13, 251–273.
Triandafyllidou, A. and Kokkali, I. (2010) *Tolerance and Cultural Diversity Discourses in Greece.* Accept Pluralism Research Project, Background Country Reports, 2010/08. Florence: European University Institute. Available at: https://ec.europa.eu/migrant-integration/?action=media.download&uuid=FBF92A50-9584-64EA-E8CBDFBCBBEBCA59 [Accessed 8 September 2020].
Triandafyllidou, A. and Maroukis, T. (2010) *Migration in 21st Century Greece.* Athens: Kritiki [in Greek].
United Nations (2018) Global Compact on Safe, Orderly and Regular Migration. Available at: www.un.org/en/ga/search/view_doc.asp?symbol=A/RES/73/195 [Accessed 8 September 2020].
Veronis, L. (2014) Somali Refugees Show How Conflict, Gender, Environmental Scarcity Become Entwined. Available at: www.newsecuritybeat.org/2014/08/experience-somali-refugees-shows-conflict-gender-environmental-scarcity-entwined [Accessed 8 September 2020].
Verweij, M. and Thompson, M. (2006) *Clumsy Solutions for a Complex World: Governance, Politics and Plural Perceptions.* London: Palgrave.
Vullnetari, J. and King, R. (2009) *Albanian Migration, Remittances and Development: A Gendered Perspective.* UNDP-INSTRAW project 'Gender and

Remittances: Creating Gender-Responsive Local Development'. Brighton: Sussex Centre for Migration Research, University of Sussex.

William, A. and Baláž, V. (2012) Migration, Risk, and Uncertainty: Theoretical Perspectives. *Population Space and Place* 18 (2), 167–180.

Winters, N. and Izaguirre Mora, C. (2019). Es cosasuya: Entanglements of Border Externalization and African Transit Migration in Costa Rica. *Comparative Migration Studies*, 7 (27), 1–20.

World Bank (2015) *Country Partnership Framework for Albania 2015–2019*. Washington DC: World Bank. Available at: www.worldbank.org/en/country/albania/publication/albania-country-partnership-framework-2015#:~:text=The%20World%20Bank%20Group's%20new%20Country%20Partnership%20Framework%20for%20Albania,public%20services%20for%20its%20citizens [Accessed 8 September 2020].

World Bank (2016). Growth Continues in Albania as Employment Improves in the Region. Press release, 27 September. Available at: www.worldbank.org/en/news/press-release/2016/09/27/growth-continues-in-albania-as-employment-improves-in-region [Accessed 08 September 2020].

Zickgraf, C. (2018) Immobility. In: McLeman, R. and Gemenne, F. (eds) *Routledge Handbook of Environmental Displacement and Migration*. London: Routledge, pp. 71–84.

3 Return mobilities of first-generation Albanians

Reconciling the rupture of disintegration and negotiating the future

Introduction

In Chapter 2 we discussed the links between return migration, reintegration, and onward mobility (whether of remigration, or circular/ transnational migration) taking into account particularly the type and duration of return (whether occasional, periodic/seasonal, temporary or permanent), the level of preparedness (non-existent, low, or medium), and the level of reintegration (non-existent/refusal, partial, low, medium) that ensues. Our reflections arise from a review of both the relevant literature and the specific migration system of Albania, Italy, and Greece, and its specific features. In this chapter we focus on first-generation migrants, notably people who were born in Albania and moved to Greece or Italy at a certain point in their life (as adults), and then returned to Albania (those born at destination 'returning' to Albania are discussed in Chapter 4). This chapter starts with an overall thick description of our sample population, looking at their main socio-demographic features and their situation of return, reintegration, or onward mobility at the time of our fieldwork in 2014 and 2017.

After this general overview, the chapter follows the return–reintegration– mobility experience in a chronological sequence. We first analyse the motivations and preparations for returning (hence the pre-departure stage from the destination country), the type – intentions and duration – of return, and then the post-return and reintegration phase. In this last phase we distinguish between socio-economic and cultural-identity reintegration aspects. The last section of the chapter discusses remigration and onward mobility patterns.

The dynamics analysed in this chapter investigate the relationship between preparedness for return (real and perceived), return and decisions (or concrete plans) for staying, remigrating and/or engaging in circular or transnational mobility. We consider reintegration as a potential for both onward migration or settlement in the country of origin and look at the decisive factors that eventually lead to leaving or staying. We also look at the relationship between return and engaging in mobility (either circular or transnational), investigating the importance of structural factors like employment opportunities and migration restrictions (or available options), but also of cultural and social factors like networks in both countries and feelings of belonging to either. In short, we explore the extent to which return and reintegration can breed a transnational living, whether by choice or by necessity. We also pay attention to the gender dimension throughout the study looking at how gender impacts plans and opportunities for return, remigration, or circularity, as well as to the urban vs rural divide, given that earlier studies suggest different strategies of internal migration or remigration for cities and rural areas.

The socio-demographic profile of the sample

While both countries of destination, Italy and Greece, have registration procedures in place that allow assessment of the number of regular migrants, estimates of return migrants are far from reliable. There are typically no robust statistical procedures that could register Albanians who leave Greece or Italy to return to Albania. Of course, this could find explanation in the diverse constellation of national and EU rules in place as well as the policies and fluidity of legal statuses (e.g. dual nationality, long-term residence permit, visa liberalization regime, or irregularity) that cut across national borders and institutional competencies. When it comes to the country of origin and its responsibility towards its citizens, despite improvements in the management of migration and reintegration policies, in Albania the existing procedures are not yet properly adopted to keep track of return migration. Indeed, the number of returnees who registered in the national network of Migration Counters – special offices operating at the regional and local employment offices that provide services to prospective migrants, returnees, and immigrants (Albanian Ministry of Interior and IOM 2019) – are extremely limited compared to the dynamic of the reality on the ground.

In the absence of a complete data framework, our study starts with the effort of building a reliable profile of first- and second-generation returnees from Greece and Italy. The examination of their specific demographic characteristics across generations and coming from two different destination countries offers an important framework within which to discuss their patterns of return, reintegration, and mobility. Yet, by comparing return experiences of individuals from two different countries of settlement in two different time cohorts, our aim is to understand the (permanent or temporary) nature of return, its intensity, and the volatility of push and pull factors behind it as well as to whether and how it involved further mobility and what kind of mobility/onward migration.

In our study, the gender distribution of 2014's and 2017's samples is marginally balanced, with men returnees from Italy outnumbering women (Table 3.1 and Table 3.2). However, the gender distribution of 2017's sample is relatively more balanced compared to the sample of 2014 (Table 3.2). This is further corroborated by some recent estimation of the Albanian Ministry of Interior and IOM (2019) according to which 38,000 of 42,313 Albanian citizens who returned in 2016–2017 were men.

The majority of returnees of 2014's sample belong to the age category 41–50 years followed by the 31–40 age bracket (totalling

Table 3.1 Socio-demographic profile of returnees, 2014

Variables	Categories	Country		Total
		Greece	*Italy*	
Gender	*Male*	8	11	19
	Female	8	4	12
Age distribution	*20–30*	1	3	4
	31–40	5	5	10
	41–50	7	5	12
	51–60	3	2	5
Family status	*Married*	16	12	28
	Single	0	3	3
Education level	*Secondary*	14	9	23
	Tertiary	2	6	8
Length of stay	*0–10*	1	4	5
	11–20	11	11	22
	21–25	4	0	4
Year of return	*2010–2011*	3	7	10
	2012–2013	13	8	21
Type of return	*Family*	11	10	21
	Individual	5	5	10
Type of mobility	*Transnational*	4	3	7
	Circular/seasonal	0	4	4
	Re-emigration	2	2	4
Total				31

Source: authors' compilation from data collected for this study

73 per cent). This corroborates other studies' findings (Maroukis and Gemi 2013; Vullnetari 2015) showing that return migrants consist mostly of working-age adults (Table 3.1). Slightly different seems to be the involvement of a younger generation in return flows of 2017's sample, namely those who belong to age category 31–40 years (Table 3.2). In both samples, 'married' returnees outnumbered by far 'single' individuals, a very articulated demographic element embedded in Albanian migration patterns in general (Table 3.1 and Table 3.2).

Table 3.2 Socio-demographic profile of returnees, 2017

Variables	Categories	Country		Total
		Greece	**Italy**	
Gender	*Male*	5	6	11
	Female	5	4	9
Age distribution	*20–30*	0	0	0
	31–40	3	7	10
	41–50	6	1	7
	51–60	1	2	3
Family status	*Married*	9	7	16
	Single	1	3	4
Education level	*Secondary*	6	5	11
	Tertiary	4	5	9
Length of stay	*0–10*	0	3	3
	11–20	6	5	11
	21–25	4	2	6
Year of return	*2010–2011*	0	1	1
	2012–2013	5	3	8
	2014–2015	3	2	5
	2016–2017	2	5	7
Type of return	*Family*	7	3	10
	Individual	3	7	10
Type of mobility	*Transnational*	3	2	5
	Circular/seasonal	0	2	2
	Re-emigration/remigration	1	2 (Italy/France)	3
Total				**20**

Source: authors' compilation from data collected for this study

In terms of education, despite the prevalence of 'secondary' education level returnees, there is a difference between the two countries of destination. Thus, the education level of returnees from Italy seems to be far more balanced (between secondary and tertiary education) compared to those coming from Greece, whose majority consists of secondary-education level (Table 3.1). In 2017's sample the level of education appeared similar for both countries, with the number of returnees of 'secondary' education prevailing (Table 3.2).

The length of stay in country of destination is related to various stages of the migration cycle. In theory, it particularly reflects the level of integration and transnational ties affecting return intentions (Carling et al. 2015: 16). Nevertheless, the return migration of Albanians from Greece and Italy in times of crisis is, by definition, exceptional but given the frequency of similar (regional/world) crises, it is neither unique nor uncommon (Bastia 2011: 11). By saying this, the question is not simply about the length of stay *per se*, but is further related to social, political, and economic situations that migrants experienced before their return and that potentially conditioned the return process.

Interestingly, in both countries and in both samples the length of time abroad follows a similar path covering a time period spanning between 11 and 20 years, followed by a time span of 21–25 years. This denotes the long-term settlement patterns of Albanians in both countries of destination. As far as year of return is concerned, in both time cohorts it covers the period 2010–2013, which corresponds to the momentum (the shock wave) of economic crisis and its impact on the life course of Albanian migrants in both countries (Table 3.1 and Table 3.2).

As far as the year of return is concerned, in both samples for those returnees coming especially from Greece it covers the years 2012–2013, which correspond to the peak of the economic crisis in that country and impacted the life course of Albanian migrants there (Table 3.1 and Table 3.2). Meanwhile, in the 2017 sample, the returnees from Italy display a slightly different time pattern, with most respondents returning to Albania in the period 2016–2017. This presumably denotes a more gradual impact of the Italian economic crisis on the livelihoods of Albanians in that country (and potentially a higher level of preparedness for return) or it could be seen as a 'return of conservatism' (Cerase 1974: 254) for those returning after achieving their original goals. It may also signal a slow-burner effect of the overall economic downturn after the 2008 financial crisis, hence a gradual worsening of the economic and employment situation of Albanian migrants in Italy and a longer period of 'resisting' return until finally deciding for return.

As stated above, return migration might happen in the frame of transnational and circular moves between places, while considering migrants as being in the process of building their itineraries (Bonifazi et al. 2008: 289). Our study shows that a significant number of returnees in our samples are either transnational or circular/seasonal, while others were engaged in re-emigration or plan to remigrate or both (Table 3.1 and Table 3.2). Indeed, onward mobility may involve transnational economic activities and circular migration (repeated short stays) between country of origin and country of destination. As discussed in Chapter 2, transnational economic activities may include for instance petty trade, transportation, and small business activities in both countries, taking advantage of one's networks in either. Circular mobility, on the other hand, is characterized by repeated temporary stays at destination (after return), such as engaging in seasonal or temporary employment in agriculture, tourism/hospitality, or construction.

Our study shows that over half our respondents (in both samples) engage in transnational or circular/seasonal mobility after return, while others plan to re-migrate or have already re-(e)migrated before even settling for good in Albania. Of those embarking on re-emigration, there are nine cases who went back to Greece and Italy in a seemingly failed attempt to resettle there, and another who re-migrated to France and Sweden. These data point to the importance of long-term status at destination as already demonstrated by earlier studies: returnees who had acquired Greek or Italian citizenship or held a permanent/long-term stay permit at the destination country returned to Albania as they felt their migratory experience was completed (given also the negative economic prospects ahead) but retained important socio-economic ties with Greece or Italy (Mai and Paladini 2013: 52).

Turning our attention to the socio-demographic profile of second-generation returnees, in contrast to the first generation, the female respondents outnumber the male respondents (Table 3.3). As could be expected, the majority of respondents belong to the age category 19–21 years followed by the 22–24 years bracket. With regard to the type of return, 'individual' returnees for study reasons outnumber the 'family' type of return, while the level of education shows a similar trend for both countries, with the number of returnees of 'tertiary' education prevailing.

Likewise, the length of stay in both countries of destination reflects the same pattern of first-generation returnees, thus covering a span of between 17 and 22 years, while the year of return fluctuates between 2013 and 2016 which could be associated with the negative ramifications of economic crisis in both countries of destination. As individual

Table 3.3 Socio-demographic profile of second-generation returnees, 2017

Variables	Categories	Country		Total
		Greece	*Italy*	
Place of birth	Albania	6	5	11
	Greece	4	0	4
	Italy	0	1	1
Gender	Male	3	3	6
	Female	7	3	10
Age distribution	16–18	3	0	3
	19–21	5	1	6
	22–24	2	3	5
	25–27	0	2	2
Education level	Secondary	1	1	2
	Tertiary	9	5	14
Length of stay	5–10	1	3	4
	11–16	4	0	4
	17–22	5	3	8
Year of return	2011	1	2	3
	2013	4	2	6
	2014	2	1	3
	2016	3	1	4
Type of return	Family	3	3	6
	Individual	7	3	10
Type of mobility	Transnational	6	2	8
	Circular/seasonal	1	0	1
	Re-migration	5	1	6
Reason of return	Studies	8	2	10
	Family return	2	2	4
	Intimate/unemployment	0	2	2
Nationality (other than Albanian)		6	1	7
Total				**16**

Source: authors' compilation from data collected for this study

return prevails over the family type of return, the majority of those returned individually have their families in Greece (Table 3.3).

As for the type of mobility, the evidence shows a prevalence of transnational moves mainly connected with the family ties in the countries of destination, while the number of those planning to remigrate remains high, with half the respondents looking to remigrate to Germany or 'somewhere else'. Most interesting is that 11 out of 16 returnees were born in Greece and Italy – 6 and 5 respectively – while the average age of those who moved to Greece and Italy with their families ranges from six months to six years, which fits the classical definition of the second generation. Finally, almost half the respondents hold dual citizenship, with those holding Greek citizenship outnumbering those with Italian (Table 3.3).

Before returning: the interaction between macro-, meso-, and micro-level drivers

By examining the interconnectedness between return and mobility, it is assumed that return does not constitute the end of a migration cycle. It could be rather seen as part of a transnational system based on the interconnection of social, cultural, and economic relationships that cut across traditional (national) borders. A closer look at the patterns of Albanian migration to Greece and Italy, as attempted in this book, highlights the role of macro and meso factors in shaping the micro level of decision-making. Thus, the economic crisis and steep rise of unemployment particularly in the construction sector (mostly in Greece but also in Italy) along with uncertain legal status (Gemi 2017) led those who intended to settle at destination to reconsider their options and decide for return or transnational or circular mobility. Return became a strategy for coping with the dramatic impact of the economic crisis on Albanian households (Gëdeshi and de Zwager 2012: 250). Anecdotal evidence suggests that more than 220,000 people returned to Albania during the 2010s (Gemi 2019: 96). Looking at Greek data, it is estimated that nearly 120,000 non-EU nationals left the country during the period 2014–2016 alone (ELSTAT 2017). Despite the lack of reliable estimates by nationality, it appears that the negative migration balance was mainly related to the return migration of people from Albania and central-eastern European countries to their places of origin (Gemi and Triandafyllidou 2018: 6). Several studies (Gemi 2019; Gëdeshi and King 2018b; Kopliku 2019) have pointed to multiple geographical paths and ventures followed by Albanian migrants before taking the decision to return to Albania and/or go back to Greece and Italy.

The impact of the crisis is not, of course, straightforward and is shaped by the specific features of different households and their preparedness and willingness to return. Thus, for those with weak economic integration, return was probably 'forced' by the economic downturn and unemployment while for others, with a stronger economic integration at destination, return was a decision made under pressure in the fear of a further worsening of the situation. Accordingly, those who felt that they had mostly achieved their economic goals and were (at least partly) ready to develop their own small business or other economic activity in Albania, the crisis acted as a catalyst for taking the decision sooner rather than later. Some study findings (Gemi 2019) suggest Albanian households based in Greece transferred all their savings to Albania before returning through informal channels, prompted by concerns about the effects of the economic crisis on the Greek banking system (i.e. capital controls imposed in July 2015) and fear of Grexit. Thus, in subsequent years, some did return and used the money to establish their own business or buy apartments or both (ibid.: 97).

In this light, timing is one of the most crucial factors in the decision to return. Carling and Schewel (2018) distinguish five 'time' categories that exert significant influence on the decision to return: the time since migration; age at migration; biographical time; bureaucratic time; and historical time. We may argue that historical and bureaucratic time are macro-level drivers; time since migration is a meso-level factor, while age at migration and biographical time (the position of migration within the migrant's life course) are micro-level drivers shaping the specific context within which decisions are taken. In this study, the role of macro- and meso-level factors is particularly salient in shaping migrants' attitudes towards return migration either positively or negatively.

In the context of economic crisis in Greece and Italy, many migrants opted to return to their home country to escape unemployment and economic impoverishment as well as the risk of falling into irregularity; losing their job would mean a possible loss of their stay permit, if that was not of an indefinite duration. Indeed, most Albanian returnees working as dependent workers both in Greece and Italy referred to unemployment as the main reason motivating the return decision as the crisis was particularly felt in the period 2011–2013. Illustrating this, the Italian National Association of Construction Companies (ANCE 2014) estimates that from 2008 to 2013, the construction sector lost some 60,000 jobs (–16.6 per cent) At the same time, the decline in the number of issued stay permits – temporary or long-term – in 2015 concerned only some nationalities (such as Albanians) predominantly working in the construction sector in Italy (Dimitriadis 2017: 1).

This section discusses the period before returning to Albania, looking at how subjective and objective conditions of unemployment and uncertainty led our respondents' decision to return to Albanian. We look at the interaction between macro-, meso-, and micro-level drivers and distinguish between negative drivers pushing towards return because remaining was no longer viable, pivotal drivers (notably elements that could push towards either direction), and positive drivers pushing towards return as a desirable option.

Negative drivers towards return

Seven interviewees pointed to onward mobility as a temporary strategy or a plan that they developed in order to face the economic downturn. Such onward mobility involved temporary onward migration to a third EU country and Canada as one strategy, albeit conditions were dire and uncertainty became particularly taxing:

> My husband worked in the construction sector with a group of Albanians who undertook contracts in the area. When the work demand fell, in order to make ends meet, he began to undertake construction works outside Italy, for example he worked for two months in Ostrava [Czech Republic] in awful conditions. Frustrated by uncertainty he insisted that we should return to Albania.
> (IT-23)

For those based in Greece such temporary or more long-term onward mobility was more complicated because of the geographical distance between Greece and third countries with vibrant economies like Germany. Interestingly Albanian households had the necessary networks to help their onward migration plan but not the necessary human capital (notably language knowledge):

> We were preparing to go to Germany. We had acquaintances there. We were told that with our profession we would find a good job with good money. But it didn't happen because my husband didn't want it because of the language. None of us knew German.
> (GR-19)

In several cases, protracted unemployment led not only to impoverishment but also to losing legal status:

> I haven't had a job in the last two years, two to three daily wages a week. For a few months I didn't work at all ... I lost my papers. I no longer had a contract for the renewal of resident permit.
> (IT-24)

The same pattern was detected in both Italy and Greece, as men experienced unemployment in the construction sector and status precarity. There was a significant wave of male returnees from Greece (Galanxhi et al. 2014), with their spouses being 'reluctant returnees' (Morokvasic 2014: 368) following them to Albania. Gemi (2016) too observed that women preferred to stay in Greece despite the difficult conditions they might face.

> The last year and a half before our return, my husband hardly worked at all. I was the only who kept working ... We exhausted all our savings. In the summer of 2013, we went for vacation in Lezha. My brother-in-law introduced my husband to a contractor who hired him for a construction work. He accepted immediately. He made the decision on behalf of all of us without asking me first. I returned to Greece with my three children. I had no papers because I was dependent from my husband. We packed our things and in 2 weeks we returned to Albania so that the children could enrol in school.[1]
> (GR-18)

The reasons behind this resistance are linked, firstly, to the fact that the majority of Albanian women continued to work and adapt to new terms and conditions in the domestic work sector and, secondly, their concerns about their children's adaptation to the reality of Albania (Gemi 2016). In many cases, amidst the economic crisis in Greece women became the main income providers for their families:

> Over the last three years, my husband worked very little. And when he worked, his daily wage was reduced. At the end, it didn't work out with my salary. When we 'ate' all the money saved, the only solution was Albania. It was not easy.
> (IT-16)

> We started feeling the crisis after the year 2009 on. The company was delaying our salaries, the prices of goods were always getting increased. They were paying our salaries in parts. They paid us 100 euros one day, then 200 euros another day ... her salary [his wife] was not reduced, but it was the expenses which were every year increasing that affected our living there.
> (IT-10)

Those who owned their business were confronted with insurmountable difficulties, unable to keep it running.

> The decline gradually began. It made its appearance at the end of 2008. Expenses were rising and revenues were declining. We have reached the point where we cannot pay taxes. Taxes were higher than revenues.
>
> (GR-19)

> I kept trying to persuade the landlord to lower the rent a bit, but he didn't listen to anything. I told him: I sell coffee for 1.5 euros. I do not have a big profit and I cannot afford to pay this rent [1,100 euros].
>
> (GR-13)

For many (40 respondents out of 51 in total) return had not been part of their plans. They were totally unprepared and both the objective situation (of unemployment and economic decline) and their subjective perception that their lives were in Greece and Italy – even if they went back for holidays and maintained kinship ties – did not help them get prepared for return or reintegration.

> We went on vacation in Albania once a year. Usually in the summer. Apart from our family homes, we did not purchase any property and we did not think about any investment there. Our life was in Greece. I never thought about returning.
>
> (GR-18)

> If the crisis had not happened, and if we continued living as we used to before 2009–2010, I would have never returned to Albania. But since we were unemployed for about two years and only my youngest son was working, we had less income ... Given that in any case we already had legal documents, we decided to come and work here in Albania hoping that things would go better here. But still, I will return again to Italy.
>
> (IT-5)

The economic crisis and the temporary nature of the legal status that many migrants (and their family members) had were two important macro-level factors that shaped the micro-level decision-making. At the same time, meso-level factors, especially the existence of kinship and other networks of support at the country of origin, also played an important part in facilitating the decision-making and channelling the transition. Meso-level factors like the kinship networks and overall social capital acted as a pull driver:

> My husband felt very tired and couldn't see any prospects ahead. He wanted to do something of his own. In Greece this was not achievable. The financial crisis had scared him ... One day he announced to me that in a month we were leaving for Shkodra where he intended to run a fish tavern with his brothers.
>
> (GR-23)

The importance of uncertain stay status, however, cannot be overestimated: many migrants lost their status as a consequence of losing their job, resulting in whole families falling into irregularity. Faced with navigating a lengthy bureaucratic process or re-acquiring status on exceptional or humanitarian grounds was seen as particularly cumbersome and emotionally difficult. At the same time, nostalgia for the home country, along with a desire and need to enhance and forge social and personal status back home became important micro-level factors that conditioned the decision-making. Yet, de-regularization and discrimination played a role in shaping the constellation of push factors.

> There were two main reasons. First the economic situation, for which we had migrated, started to be limited. But second, what influenced me most, was the fact that I continuously felt I was a refugee, I always felt as a foreigner; no matter how long you try to adapt yourself there you never become like a native person, you do not feel yourself equal to the other.
>
> (IT-3)

Pivotal drivers for return

Family and life-cycle factors such as retirement, need to care for aging parents, children's education, and marriage constitute important 'time' elements in return migration in general and with specific reference to the case under study.

> My story resembles that of Odysseus. The life cycle closes back to the family home, back to the roots. Just as he returned to Ithaca, so I returned to Albania ... My base is my father's village near Gjirokaster. I have my vineyard. I cultivate the land ... I had serious health issues that forced me to quit my job as waiter in Athens. As I have closed 20 years of regular work in Greece, I expect at the age of 65 to get even a reduced pension.
>
> (GR-17)

> I was 35 years old single and alone. My brothers had moved to Tirana with their families. They persuaded me to go to them and get married and make my life. Through an acquaintance they found me the job here. They also found me a bride. At first, I did not want to. It seemed strange to me to marry in a blind date fashion. But in the end I liked the girl. She also had her own house in Tirana. My son was born and now I am expecting my second child.
>
> (GR-25)

According to a recent study (Gëdeshi and King 2018a) this mixed set of returnees is the largest group and accounts for 54.7 per cent of returnees in total (ibid.: 71).

Positive drivers towards return

Not all drivers towards return were negative though. There were important elements in Albania that made return attractive, given the crises at destination (particularly in Greece) as they offered incentives for reintegration into the business sector or brain gain programmes. There was certainly interest in avoiding downward mobility and rather turning the crisis into an opportunity by achieving upwards socio-economic mobility at home. Thus, macro-level elements like home ownership and savings in Albania, along with the prospect of being bosses of themselves, tipped the balance towards return.

> In 2013 we took the decision to return. We said we have money, we know the job. So, why we are not going to open something of our own. In Greece, things were difficult with the economic crisis. High unemployment. The construction sector is dead. But we were working until the moment we left. But bills and costs have risen sharply. We said let's go to Albania. It will be better. Things will have changed now. If we stayed in Greece, we would dry out the savings.
>
> (GR-20)

> In the summer of 2013, I took the decision to return to Albania. I was unemployed for more than a year. In the last three years the work in the factory had dropped dramatically. Every three months the employer fired a worker. I was the last to get fired. After 17 years of hard work, I suddenly became unemployed. Fortunately, I had bought a house and a small shop in Tirana.
>
> (GR-24)

These 'willing returnees' sought thus to capitalize on their socio-economic capital gained abroad by investing in small businesses or by seeking a better-paid job in Albania. In their recent study, Gëdeshi and King (2018a) suggest that while these returnees account for a small share (around 16 per cent), it could potentially play an important part in the economic development of Albania (ibid.: 71).

In short, like other phases of the migration process, return migration can hardly be explained by a single set of drivers, while returnees differ in their return motivation. Often the reasons behind the decision to return are ambivalent. Our analysis of the pre-departure period for our interviewees suggests that macro- and meso-level factors are crucial for defining the tipping point when the decision to return is taken by the single migrant and single household. It is also interesting that gender imbalances are marked, as both the legal status of the family depended on the job of the male breadwinner and the decision to return was largely dependent on him being long-term unemployed or underemployed and eventually taking the decision to leave. This finding is not surprising given the particular structure of Albanian migration in Greece and Italy where most women worked in the cleaning and caring sector without formal contracts – holding a stay permit as spouses – and the gendered roles prevalent in Albanian households (Gemi 2017; Maroukis and Gemi 2013; Mai and Paladini 2013).

Types of return and levels of preparedness

The return of Albanian migrants from Italy and Greece in the 2010s took place during a period of economic crisis in both destination countries. We thus feel that classical distinctions of types of returnees based on the migrants' original planning (Gmelch 1980) are inadequate. Building on recent research (King 2017) and on our analytical framework as elaborated in Chapter 2, we propose four types of return characterized by different levels of preparedness and types of reintegration and leading to different forms of mobility after return. We feel that this type of dynamic framework does justice both to the realities of Albanian migration to Greece and Italy for the reasons outlined in Chapter 2 but also better captures the fluid nature of return migration today more generally (Kuschminder 2017). We distinguish therefore among (a) occasional/seasonal/circular return; (b) temporary return; and (c) long term/permanent return. All are documented in our qualitative study at varied frequencies: 31 per cent of respondents intend to return temporarily to Albania; 20 per cent are occasional/seasonal/circular returnees; and 49 per cent see their return as permanent.

The decision to return is a socially constituted decision under the combined influence of different factors. It is usually taken within the household or extensive family context (Lang et al. 2016) even if not generally in a gender-neutral way. In this section we point to the decision-making process and the level of preparedness as they characterize each type of return; special attention is paid to the volatility of the circumstances in the destination countries, a factor that significantly impacted the preparedness of return.

It is acknowledged that willingness and readiness to return are the two fundamental elements of the return migrants' preparedness. Theoretically, willingness refers to the act of conscious decision to return on one's own initiative and in the absence of any external pressure (Cassarino 2014). Readiness to return, on the other hand, reflects the extent to which migrants have been able to mobilize the adequate tangible and intangible resources needed to prepare the ground and secure their return (ibid.: 4). Willingness and preparedness are important elements of return, regardless of whether the return is temporary or permanent as they define the time, resources, and overall context within which the return takes place.

Occasional, seasonal, and circular return

As stated above, this is the smallest category among the types of return and includes roughly 20 per cent (10 individuals out of 51) of our respondents. In fact, occasional return usually involves low-skilled or unskilled migrants (usually men) who intended to re-emigrate temporarily to the established and easily accessible destinations of Greece and Italy where they could find seasonal jobs, predominantly in the informal sector, using their family or social networks (see Maroukis and Gemi 2013).This category includes migrants who decided to go back to Greece and Italy occasionally and irregularly (as temporary visitors since a visa was no longer required to enter Schengen) to earn a living for themselves and their families.

> Everything depends on the job place. I live here only temporarily because as soon as my friends call me that they have found a job there I immediately go to Italy and after finishing my job there I return here since I have no place to live there. So, if I have no job there, I live here in Albania. The ticket of travelling by ferry from Italy to Albania is 50 euros while there in Italy you can't afford living without having a job.
>
> (IT-09)

Seasonal/circular return refers mostly to migrants who spent up to three months in Greece or Italy in a 12-month period, every year. In terms of age and gender, most seasonal and circular migrants are single men in their mid-20s or middle-aged married men. They generally came from relatively poor families, living in deprived rural areas or were internal (rural to urban) migrants settled in urban centres who could not find stable employment there and did not have any other options for regular remigration as they had lost their status in Greece or Italy (see also Vullnetari 2015: 153). This category includes men who could not keep their families in Greece or Italy because they had lost their jobs. After the family's return to Albania, the husband or father engaged in circular migration as a strategy for earning additional income or as a way to test possible avenues for further long-term remigration to a third country (see also Gemi 2016; Mai and Paladini 2013). This type of return is facilitated by a visa-free regime and well-established social networks but reshaped in terms of time and frequency because of the crisis:

> I used to go back and forth for years. In Albania, I work in my own fields and breed my own livestock. We don't get a salary or a pension. I go to Italy from time to time. Now, I will go to there in October because I have been called for work. I was told it will probably last for a month.
>
> (IT-24)

Temporary return and transnational mobility

We distinguish between seasonal/circular mobility and *temporary return*, which involves different types of transnational mobility between origin and destination. This category comprises the 31 per cent of our sample who expressed their intention to return temporarily to Albania. In other studies (Mai and Paladini 2013; Maroukis and Gemi 2013), this category included returned entrepreneurs whose base was in Albania and who travel back and forth frequently as part of their business transactions.

Temporary return is also typically a possibility for those who had acquired long-term status or citizenship but opted to engage in business at the origin country because they could not afford to keep their enterprise at destination because of high running costs.

> In the beginning, the scenario was for my husband to return to Vlora where we have our apartment, while I and my daughter to

stay in Greece and run the shop we had in Porto Rafti. In the meantime, my relatives that are very well established in Tirana, advised us to go to Tirana. They found us a [butcher] store and an apartment to rent. They helped enrol my daughter in Arsakeio.

(GR-19)

Indeed, the 2011 census data reveal the patterns linking return and internal migration with approximately 40 per cent of return migrants who decided to establish themselves in a location other than their city or village of origin, with Tirana the most preferred city (Galanxhi et al. 2014).

In other cases, the transnational mobility could also have as an objective the renewal of the husband or father's stay permit or acquisition of the long-term permit or citizenship in order to keep future options open and be able to circulate between the two countries (see also Mai and Paladini 2013: 52). Indeed, temporary return with immediate intention to re-emigrate is facilitated by permanent legal status in country of destination:

> If the crisis had not happened, and if we continued living as we used to before 2009–2010, I would have never returned to Albania. But since we were unemployed for about two years and only my youngest son was working, we had less income... given that in any case we already have legal documents, we decided to come and work here in Albania hoping that things would go better here. But still, I will return again to Italy.
>
> (IT-5)

Becoming a Greek or Italian citizen was also a strategy for obtaining and EU citizenship and possibly trying to emigration to a third EU country later (see Karamoschou 2018).

Temporary return and transnational mobility could also happen in the reverse order. The husband or father returned to Albania to find a job instead of being unemployed in Greece, while the rest of the family remained at destination.

> We are staying here temporarily because we have children and we want to help them. They are in Greece. My daughter does her internship and gets paid and my son is unemployed.
>
> (GR-4)

Family networks were mentioned by most interviewees as an important meso-level driver that shaped decisions for returning.

Resource mobilization in preparation of return involved both savings and mobilizing kinship and wider networks (which were also seen as an important element of identification, see Mai and Paladini 2013: 60).

Permanent return

Almost half of our respondents view their return to Albania as permanent. Turning to permanent return options, these include both voluntary and involuntary permanent returnees to Albania:

> When we first moved to Italy we were thinking about returning. When the children were born, we stopped worrying about returning. We didn't see it as an option. Finally, we did return in November 2016 because my husband was unemployed for a long time.
>
> (IT-16)

Those who planned for a long-term return showed a high level of preparedness and took time to mobilize the necessary resources to secure a successful return.

> In 2013, we took the decision to return. We said we have money, we know the job, let's go and run our own business.
>
> (GR-20)

This category includes migrants whose migration cycles were indeed complete, but with the time of return decided a little abruptly. They feel they had gathered adequate tangible and intangible resources to carry out their projects in their home countries, for instance having a home, social and family networks, and savings.

> From the first moment we met, my husband knew very well what he wanted. Since then, he used to say we need to buy a house and a shop in Tirana to prepare the return. From the moment that we had the money, we bought the house we are living in today.
>
> (GR-17)

> I didn't have time to think about returning. I worked a lot. The children were growing up just fine. In 2007 my brother bought an apartment in Tirana and urged me to buy another apartment near

him at a good price. At first I didn't want to but he persuaded me. Fortunately, as things turned out, I did the right thing because after our return we moved there.

(GR-24)

These returnees had evaluated the costs and benefits of return, while considering the market value of their business venture:

We were thinking to run either cafeteria or patisserie. The last one seemed better to us because we knew the job and we would cover the production ... I returned first and chose the location. I wanted a wealthy neighbourhood so people can have money and know of good quality.

(GR-11)

Several also had long-term status at destination (or citizenship) so they knew they could potentially re-emigrate or engage in transnational mobility if necessary or profitable. They had prepared meticulously, mobilizing their networks at origin and destination, maximizing not only financial resources but also information:

My mom had a trip in Albania. She met some common acquaintances and learned about the university. A friend of hers promised that if I got my degree here, she would find me a job. So my mom, without telling me anything, paid the registration fees at the department of economics and told me in October you are going there. I took my clothes, the car and went to the border. Mom had taken care of everything. She had renovated the apartment in Tirana to make me feel comfortable.

(GR-20)

Among the permanent return category, there were individuals who voluntarily returned and had a relatively high level of preparedness:

I used to come to Albania often, especially in the fall. I was helping my parents in building the house. What you see now used to be a hut my parents bought when they moved from the 'mountains' here in the city of Lezha in the early 1990s. I slowly built this restaurant and then I returned for good. We also built a small animal farm. We produce our own cheese, butter, jams, bread, and raki.

(IT-25)

In most cases (20 out of 25 respondents), however, unemployment and economic hardships led to a hasty, unplanned and unprepared return. Indeed, most respondents had intended to settle permanently in Greece or Italy, but the crisis – along with the precarious legal status at the destination – led to an abrupt return, as a failure of the migration project even if there had been some preparation. Some of the permanent returnees felt that the crisis interrupted their migration cycle; along with the low level of social capital, this did not allow them to properly mobilize tangible and intangible resources. This category of individuals considers that the costs of remaining were higher than those of returning home.

> The financial crisis along with some family problems forced us to take the decision to return. Things didn't go as we had thought and so there was no reason for us to stay in Greece anymore. In addition, my mother in Shkodra was completely alone and needed me.
>
> (GR-22)

Obviously, not all the individuals had intended to return for good, but the force of circumstances made them change their initial plans:

> Actually, our return to Albania was meant as temporary. We waited for the situation to get better in Italy, and we even went back there several times, but then I could notice that it was a waste of time and money.
>
> (IT-4)

Of course, intentions may change after arrival in the country of origin. Individuals who intended to return permanently might decide to return even in the absence of hardship, while others who intended only a temporary return, found it hard to re-emigrate:

> At the moment we returned, we didn't know yet whether we were coming back permanently or temporarily. I was just feeling unsecure because for all those years in Italy I didn't even manage to save money to buy my own house here in Albania. All I did during my whole staying in Italy was to save a certain amount of money which I spend almost all during the last two years of my staying in Italy because of the crisis.
>
> (IT-12)

I am not sure about that, since I don't know how much my job is guaranteed here. For instance, my employer might fire me and I would have nothing to do ... I have no more hopes for Italy. I mean, if I want to go, I can go since I already have legal documents, but I can't think of opportunities there since the Italians themselves are facing big economic problems and the unemployment rate is high.

(IT-4)

In such cases a low level of preparedness is noticed. This category embraces migrants whose migration cycle was incomplete regardless of their length of stay abroad. Individuals consider that the costs of remaining are higher than returning home, even if few resources were mobilized before their return. Others return with a view to reducing living costs while leaving open the option of cross-border mobility and re-emigration:

Since my husband was unemployed for two years, I thought that with the money we have it would be better to come here and try instead of just going for rent in Greece. If I do not achieve something here, I am thinking of returning to Greece again.

(GR-3)

For those returnees whose level of preparedness is non-existent, their migration cycle was abruptly interrupted. These individuals neither contemplated return, nor prepared for it as it was the circumstances in host countries which prompted them to leave:

We had no job prospects. For one year I was in the unemployment fund and at the same time worked irregularly at the Hellenic Petroleum. When this job ended and the fund was over, then I had to make a decision ... We had unpaid rent for three months. In a little while the car insurance would be over. Life had become very difficult.

(GR-10)

My wife said to me that what are we going to do, it's not worth staying in this country anymore. I remember our son was on the second grade, we decided to take our clothes, and the furniture remained in Italy.

(IT-04)

This section has illustrated the inherent difficulty of categorization of types of return and how typologies of return migration are extremely context-bounded and context-dependent. As such, they must always be referred to or build up on specific examples, otherwise they lose both their analytical and practical value. The ongoing event of economic crisis is a relevant example of circumstances which have led to a significant flow of mainly unforeseen return and blurred the analytical boundaries of existing typologies.

So far, return preparedness refers to a process that unfolds in an individual's life over time and is shaped by changing circumstances – economic crisis, personal experiences, and family issues – in destination and origin countries. What matters, however, is that regardless of length of stay, migration cycle, and subjective feelings, the decision to return was dictated mostly by external circumstances, whether objectively justified or not. As far as willingness is concerned, unexpected events and other subjective and objective obstacles disrupted the migration cycle and induced migrants to return home sooner than expected or ever planned (Cassarino 2014: 4).

Reintegration challenges and opportunities

The ongoing economic recession in two main countries of destination, Greece and Italy, forced Albanians to a rather chaotic return, which had the potential of exacerbating the difficulties of reintegration. According to Cassarino (2014: 2), the patterns of reintegration are shaped by three interconnected dimensions: the context in migrants' home country; the duration and type of migration experience; and the pre- and post-return conditions. He further argued that the optimal reintegration would occur when two preconditions are met, namely a long length of stay abroad and favourable motivations to return. In our case under study, the first precondition was met (the long-term stay abroad); however, for many interviewees the second was not since return was not voluntary but rather forced upon them. Regardless of whether their return was temporary or permanent, our study revealed that Albanian returnees faced great difficulties upon return in a number of areas, including limited job opportunities, lower standards of living, socio-political insecurity, an unstable market, and a dysfunctional public administration:

> To get VAT number you have to pay 110,000 lek when all over the world it is free. There are still problems with water supply and electricity. The life is very expensive ... We have no give and take

transaction with Albanian banks. We do everything we need with the money we brought from Greece. When we need more money, we go to Ioannina and withdraw cash from banks there.

(GR-19)

Yet, having the experience of living in relatively advanced social systems they need to become re-accustomed to norms and values that were no longer familiar. They also found themselves in an ambivalent position: while their experiences, skills, and human capital could become an added value to the country's progress and democratization, they also risked being seen as a challenge to Albania's socio-economic and political establishment.

Nevertheless, many returnees mobilized their human and social capital to improve their relationship with public administration and navigate the tricky socio-economic environment of the home country:

Albanian state gives the impression that it sees you as a tool of exploitation. I try to avoid transactions with the public administration. My papers are fine, I don't owe money. I have never taken any loan. I have made a good name for myself because I participate in cooking TV shows, I have customers from all over the country. I also keep very good relationships with journalists and so I have gained publicity.

(IT-25)

Reintegration in Albania took place in an unfavourable economic environment as the country also suffered from the consequences of the global economic crisis. According to World Bank (2015) data, average GDP growth fell to 2.5 per cent in 2009–2015, from 6.1 per cent in 2000–2008. At the same time, unemployment rose to 17.1 per cent in 2015 (33.2 per cent for those 15–29 years old) from 13.0 per cent in 2008 (Gëdeshi and King 2018a: 16). What is more crucial, the financial crisis at the two main destination countries, Italy and Greece, resulted in decreasing remittance flows into Albania that had been a vital source of finance and one of the main contributors to poverty alleviation of Albanian households since the early 1990s. While in 2007, remittances accounted for 12.3 per cent of GDP, in 2015 they dropped to 5.8 per cent of GDP (ibid.:14). Since then, remittances have recovered, reaching 8.2 per cent of GDP in 2017 and are expected to rise further with growth returning at the main destination countries of Albanian migration. The return of Albanian emigrants had a double impact on the Albanian economy as it meant both a significant reduction in remittances but also a rise in people seeking employment. Finding a stable job upon return is one of the main aspects of returnees' economic reintegration. The Gëdeshi and King (2018b) study on the status of returnees in the labour market revealed that only 13.3 per cent of returnees are self-employed, while 27.6 per cent work full-time and 6.6 per cent work part-time (ibid.: 75).

In the absence of specific reintegration measures, our research confirms the importance of strong family ties that proved crucial for returnees and made up for the lack of institutional support for reintegration:

> Especially in the beginning we didn't know the streets, the shops, the services. My aunt showed us a slaughterhouse in Fieri. A cousin of mine introduced us to a wholesaler in Gjirokaster. They helped us to find the raw material and identify the right sources ... In the beginning we had difficulties with language and the ways of communication.
>
> (GR-19)

Our respondents highlighted that expertise and high human capital were less important for reintegrating into the Albanian labour market. Social capital, the right 'connections', and a medium level of skills proved to be more crucial. As Reiner and Dragos (2012: 121) also showed, low- or semi-skilled returnees who possessed practical know-how and experience opted for self-employment, at times with great success:

> Upon our return my husband opened his own business in construction sector. He was helped by a very close friend. Although he had no formal qualifications in construction work, he was able to get a licence. He learned the job in Greece. He runs now a company with 25 staff and undertakes construction contracts.
>
> (GR-17)

Unfortunately, success stories were not very common. As earlier studies have shown (Gemi 2019; Maroukis and Gemi 2013) starting a business activity in Albania or being self-employed was often hampered by overall socio-economic instability and inadequate financial support schemes (e.g. bank loans), exacerbated by the lack of infrastructure and targeted reintegration policies. However, this study shows that such barriers were at times overcome by mobilizing skills learnt at destination and family resources, opting for small family-run businesses:

Everything my wife has learned in Greece she applies here. We run a Greek patisserie. (GR-20)

Corruption in Albania is a deterrent factor that cuts across labour market and socio-economic spheres. Moreover, it can produce a feeling of social alienation in returnees who have become accustomed to different norms and standards:

> The level of corruption is high. The economy sucks. The education system as well. In Italy I have never put my hand in the pocket for my children. Everything was free: doctors, medicines, schools. Here you have to pay for everything. You go to get a birth certificate and you pay. You go to get an ID, you pay. You even pay to enrol your children in public schools.
> (IT-20)

Lack of appropriate infrastructure and favourable political mechanisms to support the local economy remain the most challenging factors of economic reintegration. Those returning to live in villages face stagnation when trying to make use of their land (Vathi and Zajmi 2017: 38), which is also confirmed by the following respondent:

> There is no market to sell our products. There is no water for the fields. This year, with the drought, everything has been destroyed. The state nowhere, no subsidies like in Italy, nothing.
> (IT-24)

The reintegration efforts are too often followed by internal migration from peripheries to urban centres, preferably the capital Tirana, which offers better employment opportunities and a modern lifestyle:

> I couldn't imagine staying in Vlora. It is a province where the old mentality prevails. It has no market. What job could we do there?
> (IT-16).

In fact, investments in infrastructure and public services have been disproportionately focused on Tirana, contributing to the neglect of infrastructure in rural areas. At the same time even in Tirana, water and electricity supplies remain scarce and expensive (Pojani 2010: 494). In a recent study (Gëdeshi and King 2018a) more than half of the returnees reported a lack of quality services and an inadequate public health system, which along with unemployment, insufficient income, and lack of quality services are cited among the top factors for considering remigration (ibid.: 19). On top of that, upon return, migrants do not have proper access to assistance or protection – for instance, housing, employment, business start-up support, or access to education and the health system.

Even though the Albanian government has developed a migration and reintegration strategy since 2005, this remains at best inadequate. The first National Strategy on Migration and its Action Plan (2005–2010) was followed by the Action Plans on Remittances (2007–2010) and the Strategy on the Return and Reintegration of Albanian Citizens (2010–2015). Together, they form the three axes of this strategy. More recent strategic documents include the Diaspora Strategy (2018–2024) and the National Strategy on Migration for Albania 2019–2022, and the respective Action Plan. The first reintegration strategy failed to distinguish between voluntary and forced returns and focused on the necessity to improve the provision of information to prospective and actual returnees and their referral to available services (e.g. Migration Counters). While designed to offer information for public and private services available to returnees, the Migration Counters have merely played an advisory role (i.e. providing information but not concrete services) in reintegration as they lack the dedicated staff and technical know-how (Albanian Ministry of Interior and IOM 2019: 24).

The European Commission, in the 2016 Progress Report, identified the absence of a cross-sector national strategy on migration and the contradictory legal provisions as serious issues of concern. Other reports (Hackaj and Shehaj 2017) pinpoint problems with the lack of data on the number of returnees and the lack of trust in the services provided by public institutions (ibid.: 50). For instance, the National Strategy on Migration for Albania 2019–2022 acknowledges the importance of removing barriers to the recognition of degrees, qualifications, and skills gained abroad as a crucial factor for the sustainable reintegration of returnees and for addressing skills shortages in the labour market (Albanian Ministry of Interior and IOM 2019: 24). However, as our study reveals, the highly skilled individuals (i.e. university graduates) met great difficulties in finding a salaried job and opted for self-employment venues:

> The infrastructure is far from functional as in Italy ... In Albania there is a great weakness and it is not just that employers give you void promises but they give you guarantees for something that does not exist ... I insist to the prospect of doing something of my own in the sector of tourism.
> (IT-19)

While economic reintegration is particularly challenging, returnees find it easier to adjust to the home country as they can tap into their wider family and kinship networks. These of course come with a price, as any new habits or customs they may bring or a different way of life to which they became accustomed abroad might create tensions and misunderstandings (Carling et al. 2015: 30). Bringing new ideas and lifestyles, returnees often find themselves at odds with the local culture. In a few cases, a specific sort of discrimination along class and social background lines makes the reintegration process even more complicated, while producing a feeling of social alienation in return:

> People's mentality is strange. I feel like a dual stranger. First, because I am the Greek and secondly because I am a provincial. I have never seen more racism for the provincials than in Tirana. There are entire neighbourhoods in Tirana like ghettos with inhabitants having come from a specific area of Albania. The 'Tiranians' call them 'Chechens', meaning uncivilized.
>
> (GR-25)

Reintegration becomes even more problematic when the return implies resurgence of gender inequalities:

> In other words, I am the cheesemaker [family business]. I see myself lost and trapped in a backward environment. In Greece I had my job [domestic cleaner], my independence, my social contacts. I felt like a decent human being.
>
> (GR-18)

Sometimes returnees typically face great expectations from people in their community of origin and risk being regarded as failures. Studies (Mema et al. 2019: 27) show that return may be positive because of capital investment and new ideas but may have a negative connotation associated with the idea that return has come as a result of failure, retirement, or nostalgia:

> Upon return you just realize that you have been missing for a long time and your name is no longer on the list. You are claiming your position from the beginning. Returning is never easy. Many people tell you 'look, the Greek is coming' and see you with a derogatory look, as a failure.
>
> (GR-26)

However, depending on the point in their life cycle, for many returnees reinserting themselves into familial and familiar networks can make them feel at home and socially empowered:

> Albania is a rather problematic country, full of contradictions. Nothing is self-evident or predictable. However, I feel at home. I open the door and meet friends. I drink coffee and raki with them. I go to the theatre. I walk.
>
> (IT-17)

Strangely enough, although Albania has concluded several agreements with other countries on social protection of Albanian citizens which guarantee the portability of pensions along with other social security benefits, there are no similar agreements with Greece or Italy. Given the dynamic of return and mobility, the need for such agreements with these two countries (which host approximately 70 per cent of Albanian migration) is emphasized in the National Strategy for the Diaspora (2018–2024). Whether it can be achieved remains to be seen in the near future.

Return, circulation, and transnational mobility

Returning to Albania for many individuals is an event characterized by insecurity, reintegration problems, disappointment, and complex challenges. Many returnees opt for occasional, seasonal/circular or temporary return in order to be able to sustain themselves and their families in a context of socio-economic fragility and employment precarity (Mai and Paladini 2013: 53). Indeed, return is usually only a step in a longer migration project and is closely connected with forms of circular mobility, transnational activity, and remigration. In the era of globalization, it is important to project human mobility as continuous process and draw a distinction between return as the 'end of journey' and return as an additional chain in a 'transnational way of being' (Levitt and Glick Schiller 2004).

The migration system of Albania, Italy, and Greece under study in this book bears witness to a world where mobility is becoming a way of life and where migration patterns are circular, multi-causal, and interdependent, with the effects of change in one part of the system being traceable through the rest of the system (Faist 1998).

Return and transnational mobility

Post-return mobility takes place within a context of close economic and social ties, strong transnational networks, a favourable visa regime (visa liberalization since 2010), and, for many, legal status in both countries (holding citizenship at both origin and destination or holding at least long-term status at the destination country). In addition, new information and communication technologies facilitate a transnational life and make separation more bearable (Lowell and Findlay 2001: 15). Our study has revealed several forms of transnational mobility where the family may be based in both countries:

> The rest of my family is in Athens. We had bought a small apartment in Sepolia where my wife and daughter actually live. We are still paying the instalments of the loan, which is why my wife continues to work in Athens. There are many difficulties, but still no big deal. The two countries are so close.
>
> (GR-26)

Such transnationalism is motivated by economic reasons but also by a wish to explore the potential of both countries and make the most of one's transnational experience and networks:

> In fact, only I have temporarily returned in Albania. Last year I started a film production business with my daughter which is based in Tirana. In Italy this is impossible. You need a lot of money. My latest film *Broken* was a project co-financed by Albanian and Italian Cinema Centres. I go to Rome every 4–5 months, stay for 1 month and come back to Tirana again. My daughter comes to Tirana often and especially when we have to submit a funding project because the production company is in her name.
>
> (IT-17)

> I go to Italy every 2–3 months to visit my children. I stay there for 1–2 weeks and come back to Shkodra. Children's lives continue normally in Italy. Every month I send them 400–500 euros. My wife and I have *carta di soggiorno*. As soon as the children turn 18, they will receive Italian citizenship.
>
> (IT-20)

Further, acknowledging the circularity and complexity of return and remigration in the context of Albanian migration in Greece and Italy, return migration should be incorporated as an episode in long-term complex migration trajectories (Lang et al. 2016: 11):

> My younger son is here now. He worked for a while in Italy with his brother but then he lost his job and so he is staying longer here till the next call for job. The older son works in summer season in Giulianova. He gets 1,200 euros a month. Ever since I came back from Italy, our children have been taken care of us.
>
> (IT-24)

Such complex return and transnational mobility patterns and potential remigration appear sustainable both culturally and economically but are at odds with official policies (which define sustainable return as 'the absence of migration after return because the returnee is fully integrated socially and economically in the home country'. ACP Observatory on Migration and IOM 2013: 13.

Seasonal and circular migration patterns after return

Seasonal or circular mobility after return reconfirm the proverb that nothing is more permanent than temporary migration (Vullnetari 2015: 147). Circular migration is a well-established pattern especially between Greece and Albania. As Morokvasic (2003) emphasizes, circular migration demonstrates the complexity of migratory processes as migrants 'settle in mobility' (ibid.: 113). Circular migration between Greece and Albania or Italy and Albania includes trans-border and short-term movements, regular and undocumented, for the purpose of work and trade (Fokkema et al. 2016). In this back–and–forth movement, the migrant spends up to three months per year in each country:

> At the end of 2013 we [his family] returned for good. Since then I am coming and going because I do not have a permanent job. When they call me, I went and worked there for three months. I used to go back and forth again and again.
>
> (GR-14)

Of course, the proximity of countries is significant in circular migration, allowing migrants to follow back-and-forth trajectories between two countries as the main reason is to work but not settle in a neighbouring country (Morokvasic 2003). Indeed, in the case at hand – before and after the 2008 economic crisis – in the absence of viable regular migration channels, circular migration has been a common pattern for low- and semi-skilled Albanian migrants working in Greece and Italy on a seasonal basis. Although intended only for tourism, the Schengen arrangements have, on the one hand, facilitated circular movements, and on the other, have had a negative impact on the informal employment of Albanians in the labour market of Greece and Italy.

In fact, the circular and transnational movements for seasonal, often informal, employment in specific sectors of the economy (e.g. agriculture and tourism) are known as the most frequent means by which the migration of Albanians to Greece and Italy has been developed since 1990s. Evidence from the IRMA project on irregular migration (Gemi 2016) showed that a significant number of Albanians reconsider their stay in either country and many are heading back to Albania or moving towards other industrial countries of western Europe with the aim of finding employment opportunities there:

> I want to go to America. I have applied for US [diversity] lottery many times but so far nothing. If the opportunity arises. I will take the children and my wife and leave. Last year I was thinking of going to Germany but those who went there were forcefully returned. I do not want my family to get exposed to another adventure.
>
> (GR-25)

However, it should be acknowledged that the economic crisis has impacted migrant categories differently. In the case of Italy, employment opportunity and legal status are, respectively, the first and second most important variables in a migrant's decision to stay put, migrate, return, or circulate (Mai and Paladini 2013: 53). In addition, Albanian migrants in the process of renewing their residence permit tended to either stay put in Greece and Italy or to 'go circular' (in the event they had to return to Albania) in order not to lose the benefits and advantages they had accumulated in relation to their legal status. On the other hand, migrants with Greek and Italian citizenship or a long-term residence permit (άδεια διαμονής and *carta di soggiorno*) tended to either stay put in Greece, Italy, or in Albania, depending on their job status as well as economic and family conditions:

> Despite the fact that I get a good pension from the Italian state [her husband died in a work accident], I was thinking about my child's future. In 2016 I went to Italy to renew the resident permit and I decided to stay. So in June 2016 I managed to convince my son to come with me on the pretext that we need to renew the papers. This time we went to Germiniano, I immediately found a job in a hospital and my son enrolled in a cookery school.
>
> (IT-22)

Particularly interesting in this respect is the fact that their return was not a conscious or pre-planned decision, but rather, a 'forced' one as the result of the exceptional economic and political situation in Greece and Italy. As such, they never gave up the social and professional ties with their society of destination, leaving a door open to re-emigrate as soon as the tide turned.

> For the moment, I am in Albania, but considering the grim prospect of this country, it would be never too late to go back to Italy ... I have a permanent residence permit (*permesso di soggiorno*), which allows me to live and work there. After 8–10 years living in Italy, when you have worked and lived legally, you have paid taxes regularly, if they need work, they are more inclined to take you at work than a new person they don't know.
>
> (IT-01)

Clearly, the decision to migrate (or to stay) is taken mostly at hoc, which in turn means that it is not irreversible. As noted here, more than half of returnees stated that they would migrate again if necessary – to Greece or Italy or elsewhere. Others had a prior experience of mobility before taking the decision to return Albania. Another highly 'mobile' group is the Albanian scientific diaspora moving from one destination country to another, with the final destination being other European countries (UK, Germany, France, the Netherlands), the USA, or Canada.

> Not in Greece. I would like to go to America. My son is preparing the papers to go to study in America. I have relatives there who are helping us with the papers.
>
> (GR-20)

Interestingly, Greece and Italy were the first host countries, serving as a starting point on the migrants' journey towards other countries (Gëdeshi and King 2018a: 37). As Gëdeshi and King support, in the trajectory from first country of settlement to final destination country, Italy and Greece lost 10.9 and 7.9 per cent of highly skilled migrants (most of them studied there) whereas the USA and Canada gained 10.1 and 4.2 per cent, respectively (ibid.: 37).

> I have planned to go to Canada ... Now I want to try another way through a labour office in Tirana where I intend to go and apply

there for going to Canada with my whole family. We tried even other ways just to leave Albania.

(IT-14)

Today, after almost three decades of migration experience and, in the context of the economic crisis in Greece and Italy, the options of return, transnational, circular migration, and re-migration become ever-more pertinent in the agenda of the Albanian migrant household. In this context, the interplay and interconnectedness between staying put and mobility schemes unfolds regardless of the lack of targeted re-integration or integration policies at home and in host countries.

Remigration

Today, emigration of Albanian citizens, especially to European Union (EU) countries, continues despite the constant improvement of living conditions in Albania, a net stable growth of the economy, and constant improvement of public safety (RoA 2017). The top factors influencing emigration towards the EU according to INSTAT (RoA 2017) include the opportunity to work abroad (84 per cent) and family reunification (4.6 per cent), followed by unemployment rates in Albania (4.2 per cent), and opportunity to study abroad (3.5 per cent). It is not a coincidence that Gallup's latest worldwide survey, conducted between 2015 and 2017, shows that in Albania, 60 per cent of the adult population wants to leave the country – ranking it fourth out of 152 countries whose citizens express a desire to migrate (Gallup 2018). The same survey puts Albania at the top of Europe on the 'brain drain' index, which measures the number of young, highly educated people who want to leave the country with no plan to return. Experts consider unemployment, low wages, rampant corruption, lack of rule of law, and lack of opportunities for upward mobility as the main reasons behind those (re)migration trends (Gëdeshi and King 2018a).

Other studies (Gëdeshi and King 2018b; Gemi 2019; Vathi and Zajmi 2017) argue that the majority of those who have chaotically returned from Greece and Italy have not achieved their migration goals and intend to realize them by re-migrating. Interestingly, a survey conducted by Gëdeshi and King (2018b) shows that more than half of returnees from Italy and almost half of returnees from Greece intend to migrate to the previous migration country (ibid.: 51), while the rest of returnees prefer other destination countries such as Germany, the USA, and the UK (ibid.: 72). However, compared to 2007 (before the global crisis of 2008) it seems that both Italy and Greece, once traditional destinations for Albanian migration, are not attractive destinations as a result of economies and a financial sector hard-hit by recession as well as prolonged high unemployment:

> I want to leave, to go to America. At least there your work is rewarded. You have no financial security here in Albania. You make an investment and no one knows what will happen.
> (GR-20)

For obvious reasons, 're-(e)migration routes' are shaped by the existence of social networks. Having relatives and friends or a previous migration experience in a country and speaking its language increases the likelihood of re-migration. This explains why Italy and Greece remain high on the list of preferred destination countries for potential Albanian migrants. The same study shows that the percentage of potential migrants who choose Italy and Greece because of the presence of social networks is higher than average; family reunification was second highest (Gëdeshi and King 2018b: 59).

Having the possibility to reconsider migration makes return much more appealing. Consequently, a high level of integration in both countries (i.e. citizenship, long-term stay permit) can facilitate return to the country of origin or re-migration to the previous host country or elsewhere. Available data show that Albanian migrants from Greece re-emigrate to Germany, the UK, North America and other EU countries without previously returning temporarily to Albania (ibid.:73). In addressing the crucial question about whether there is any relation between return and remigration, the same survey shows that 70.7 per cent of returnees aged 18–40 years wish to leave the country. An important finding corroborating our approach is that the percentage of those who have a previous migration experience is notably higher than those who haven't migrated at all (ibid.: 71).

Re-emigration to the destination country is naturally shaped by the existence of strong networks that can help with finding a job but may also be hampered if the legal conditions are not in place:

> In 2014, in the midst of great frustration and despair, I made a phone call in Athens, to one of my ladies in whose house I used to work. She told me she still needed me because the Russian lady who worked at her house would leave. I took my daughter and my younger son and I go back to Alimos. I immediately found a home and started working. My daughter started primary school and I enrolled my son in EPAL. I was really happy. I didn't get much,

about 800 euros. But it was enough for me make a living. But it was not written for me to stay in Greece. My husband threatened to divorce me if I stayed there for good. But what really made me to come back to Albania for good were the papers. I couldn't renew the papers because I was on my husband's papers. In other words, I was a protected member and since my husband did not work and did not have an income in Greece, my papers could not be renewed. That's why I decided to return again in Lezha.

(GR-18)

Intending or considering re-emigration is an important factor for maintaining transnational ties with the countries that migrants have returned from. According to respondents, most stay in touch with their friends and former employers:

The fabric production company in Florence – where I worked – supplies us with the fabrics you see. My relationship with the president of the company is very good. In fact, I have been told that if I decide to return, I will always have a place there.

(IT-16)

Concluding remarks

According to World Bank (2015) data, Albania has produced 1,438,300 migrants, equivalent to 45.4 per cent of the population residing in Albania. The scale and demographic selectivity of the outflow (mainly young individuals) has taken away part of the most active age group. Furthermore, the economic crisis that hit Greece and Italy, the two main host countries of Albanian migrants, from 2008 through the mid-2010s had several effects in terms of potential migration trends: a decrease in the inflow of out-migration, an increase in return migration, and the emergence of new (re)migration routes (onward migration) of crisis-affected Albanian migrants in Greece and Italy moving to other countries of the EU and North America to find better economic prospects (Karamoschou 2018).

Indeed, the return of Albanians from Greece and Italy has been a dynamic process, peaking twice in the last decade: in 2009–2013, and in 2016–2018 (Gëdeshi and King 2018b: 65). The return of Albanian migrants in 2009–2013 is related to the global economic crisis and the resultant high unemployment levels in Greece and Italy. However, it should be noted that from 2017 onward both Greece and Italy have entered the path of economic stability, with overall growth and employment rates gradually improving (Gemi and Triandafyllidou 2019).

This chapter began with an analysis of the reasons and motivations of return, followed by unpacking of the level of return preparedness. It then explored various forms of 'return mobilities' as well as constraints on their mobility that returnees faced before, during, and after relocating to their homeland. Indeed, mobilities appear crucial not only to the actual realization of the return process, but as directly affecting the outcomes of return. One of the main tenets is the finding that the precarious circumstances prevailing in Albania, on one hand, and access to and experience of migration is key to reintegration or re-(e)migration of returnees, making the homeland an 'optional home' (Vathi 2017). Furthermore, it became clear that circular/seasonal migration as well as transnational mobilities are a used as coping strategies of both individuals and households to face the post-return challenges and negotiate their stay or onward migration. Indeed, for those returnees who hold 'enabling citizenships' (Porobic 2017) or long-term residence permits, return is experienced as open-ended and available options perceived as enabling them to embark on further mobility, either in their former host countries or in other EU countries. Time upon return and participation in return decision-making also appears to play an important role in constituting experiences of adjustment, adaptation, and further mobility (Vathi 2017: 12). Furthermore, the degree of integration (or assimilation) in the host country is of paramount relevance to the overall experience of reintegration upon return.

The findings show that returnees were mainly individuals who lost their jobs in Greece and Italy and to a lesser extent those who came back with a plan to invest in Albania. Furthermore, most of the returnees are not those who return at the end of the migration project, but rather they are often individuals and whole families whose migration journey was disrupted by the economic crisis (Mema et al. 2019: 27). Indeed, the impact of the economic crisis along with both liberalization of the entry visa for Albanian citizens to the EU and establishment of long-term resident status, has given a new dynamic to the (dis)integration and circular/transnational mobility nexus. However, the ability of Albanians to participate in circular and transnational practices has been triggered, generating multiple and dynamic ties between migrants and their host and home countries (Gemi 2019).

Meanwhile, mobility patterns differ across the two countries. One factor that contributes to differences is the situation with regard to regularization and residence permits. In Greece, difficulties with papers have obstructed mobility to Albania and other countries. In fact, the incomplete legislative framework and the persistent refusal to accept the transformation of the country into a pole of attraction for migrants that characterized the first phase of Albanian migration (1991–1998) led to the long-term irregular stay and employment of Albanians, whereby circular (irregular) movements became the norm. However, certain political developments such as the liberalization of entry visas for Albanian citizens entering the EU, the economic crisis, and the strong tendency of de-regularization that followed, as well as the uncertain status of the second generation, caused a cascade of events related to return, the increase of transnational/circular mobility, and the search for other migratory destinations. The result of these developments is the creation of a particular category of migrants who constantly move between two countries.

Clearly, this chapter shows that the attitude towards return has been primarily developed through a transnational understanding and evaluation of opportunities in both home and host country. As such, the findings offer significant evidence on how return does not constitute the end of a migration cycle but rather an episode in the process of transnational transfers whose intentions are shaped by changing circumstances (e.g. personal experiences, contextual factors in sending country) and strongly influenced by transnational life opportunities (Nadler et al. 2016: 361).

Note

1 Frustrated by the situation in Albania, combined with the lack of integration of their three children in Albania, in winter 2018 they decided to return to Athens.

References

ACP Observatory on Migration and IOM (2013) South–South Return Migration: Challenges and Opportunities. Background Note ACPOBS/2013/BN09. Available at: https://publications.iom.int/system/files/pdf/return_migration_en.pdf [Accessed 8 September 2020].

Albanian Ministry of Interior and IOM (2019) The National Strategy on Migration and Action Plan 2019–2022. Available at: https://albania.iom.int/sites/default/files/publication/STRATEGJIA_KOMB%C3%8BTARE_ok.pdf [Accessed 8 September 2020].

ANCE (2014) *Rapporto congiunturale sull'industria delle costruzioni in Lombardia* [*Economic Report on the Construction Industry in Lombardy*]. ANCE Lombardia, Direzione Affari Economici e Centro Studi. Available at: www.lombardia.ance.it/docs [Accessed 8 September 2020].

Bastia, T. (2011) Migration as Protest? Negotiating Gender, Class, and Ethnicity in Urban Bolivia. *Environment and Planning A*, 43, 1514–1529.

Bonifazi, C., Okólski, M., Schoorl, J., and Simon, P. (eds) (2008) *International Migration in Europe: New Trends and New Methods of Analysis*. Amsterdam: Amsterdam University Press.

Carling, J. and Schewel, K. (2018) Revisiting Aspiration and Ability in International Migration. *Journal of Ethnic and Migration Studies*, 44 (6), 945–963.

Carling, J., Bolognani, M., Bivand Erdal, M., Tordhol Ezzati, R., Oeppen, C., Paasche, E., Vatne Pettersen, S., and Heggli Sagmo, T. (2015) *Possibilities and Realities of Return Migration*. PRIO Project Summary. Oslo: PRIO.

Cassarino, J. P. (2014) A Case for Return Preparedness. In: Battistella, G. (ed.) *Global and Asian Perspectives on International Migration*, Global Migration Issues 4, pp. 153–166. Berlin: Springer.

Cerase, F. (1974) Expectations and Reality: A Case Study of Return Migration from the United States to Southern Italy. *The International Migration Review*, 8, 245–262.

ELSTAT (2017) Estimated Population and Migration Flows of the Country 2016. Available at:www.statistics.gr/documents/20181/2750153/%CE%A5%CF%80%CE%BF%CE%BB%CE%BF%CE%B3%CE%B9%CE%B6%CF%8C%CE%BC%CE%B5%CE%BD%CE%BF%CF%82+%CE%A0%CE%BB%CE%B7%CE%B8%CF%85%CF%83%CE%BC%CF%8C%CF%82+%CE%BA%CE%B1%CE%B9+%CE%9C%CE%B5%CF%84%CE%B1%CE%BD%CE%B1%CF%83%CF%84%CE%B5%CF%85%CF%84%CE%B9%CE%BA%CE%AD%CF%82+%CE%A1%CE%BF%CE%AD%CF%82+%CF%84%CE%B7%CF%82+%CE%A7%CF%8E%CF%81%CE%B1%CF%82+%28+2016+%29.pdf/e58868ec-2565-4eff-9eb6-6e07d217b31e?version=1.0&t=1515658846807&download=true [Accessed 8 September 2020].

Dimitriadis, I. (2017) 'Asking Around': Immigrants' Counterstrategies to Renew Their Residence Permit in Times of Economic Crisis in Italy. *Journal of Immigrant and Refugee Studies*, 16 (3), 275–292.

Faist, T. (1998) Transnational Social Spaces Out of International Migration: Evolution, Significance and Future Prospects. *Archives Européennes de Sociologie* 39 (2), 213–247.

Fokkema, T., Cela, E., and Witter, Y. (2016) Pendular Migration of the Older First Generations in Europe: Misconceptions and Nuances. In: Horn, V. and Schweppe, C. (eds) *Transnational Aging: Current Insights and Future Challenges*. Abingdon: Routledge, pp. 141–162.

Galanxhi, E., Nesturi, M., and Hoxha, R. (2014) *Shqipëri, Popullsia dhe Dinamikat e Saj – Horizonte te Reja Demografike?* [*Albania, Population and Its Dynamics – New Demographic Horizons?*]. Tirana: INSTAT.

Gallup (2018) More Than 750 Million Worldwide Would Migrate If They Could. 10 December. Available at: https://news.gallup.com/poll/245255/750-million-worldwide-migrate.aspx [Accessed 24 December 2020].

Gëdeshi, I. and de Zwager N. (2012) Effects of the Global Crisis on Migration and Remittances in Albania. In: Sirkeci, I., Cohen, J. H., and Ratha, D. (eds) *Migration and Remittances during the Global Financial Crisis and Beyond*. Washington, DC: The World Bank, pp. 237–254.

Gëdeshi, I. and King, R. (2018a) *Research Study on Brain Gain: Reversing Brain Drain with Albanian Scientific Diaspora*. Tirana: UNDP.
Gëdeshi, I. and King, R. (2018b) *New Trends in Potential Migration from Albania*. Tirana: Friedrich-Ebert-Stiftung. Available at: http://library.fes.de/pdf-files/bueros/albanien/15272.pdf [Accessed 8 September 2020].
Gemi, E. (2016) Integration and Transnational Mobility in Time of Crisis: The Case of Albanians in Greece and Italy. *Studi Emigrazione*, LIII (202), 237–255.
Gemi, E. (2017) Albanian Migration in Greece: Understanding Irregularity in Time of Crisis. *European Journal of Migration and Law*, 19 (1), 12–33. doi: doi:10.1163/15718166-1234211.
Gemi, E. (2019) *Integration and Transnationalism in a Comparative Perspective: The Case of Albanian Immigrants in Vienna and Athens*. Vienna: Verlag der Österreichischen Akademie der Wissenschaften.
Gemi, E. and Triandafyllidou, A. (2018) *Migration in Greece: Recent Developments in 2018*. Report prepared for the Network of International Migration Experts. Paris: OECD.
Gemi, E. and Triandafyllidou, A. (2019) *Migration in Greece: Recent Developments in 2019*. Report prepared for the Network of International Migration Experts. Paris: OECD.
Gmelch, G. (1980) Return Migration. *Annual Review of Anthropology*, 9, 135–159.
GoA (2018) *The National Strategy on Migration Governance and Action Plan 2019–2022*. Tirana: Government of Albania.
Hackaj, A. and Shehaj, A. (2017) Disconnected: Return from Germany and Reintegration Challenges of Albanian Asylum Seekers. Available at: http://cdinstitute.eu/wp-content/uploads/2018/02/Disconnected.pdf [Accessed 8 September 2020].
INSTAT and IOM (2014) *Return Migration and Reintegration in Albania 2013*. Tirana: INSTAT/IOM. Available at www.instat.gov.al/media/2965/return_migration_and_reintegration_in_albania_2013_.pdf [Accessed 8 September 2020].
INSTAT and World Bank (2015) *Albania: Trends in Poverty 2002–2005–2008–2012*. Tirana: INSTAT.
Karamoschou C. (2018) *The Albanian Second Migration: Albanians Fleeing the Greek Crisis and Onward Migrating to the UK*. Sussex Centre for Migration Research Working Paper No. 93. Brighton: University of Sussex.
King, R. (2017) *Return Migration and Development: Theoretical Perspectives and Insights from the Albanian Experience*. Keynote lecture to the 2nd Annual Conference of the Western Balkans Migration Network – 'Migration in the Western Balkans: What Do We Know?', Sarajevo, 19–20 May.
Kopliku, B. (2019) Re-adjustment in the home country – the effects of return migration and transnationalism. *Research in Social Change*, 11 (1), 42–61.
Kuschminder, K. (2017) Interrogating the Relationship between Remigration and Sustainable Return. *International Migration*, 55 (6), 107–121.

Lang, T., Glorius, B., Nadler, R., and Kovács, Z. (2016) Introduction: Mobility Against the Stream? New Concepts, Methodological Approaches and Regional Perspectives on Return Migration in Europe. In: Nadler, R., Kovács, Z., Glorius, B., and Lang, T. (eds) *Return Migration and Regional Development in Europe. Mobility Against the Stream.* Basingstoke: Palgrave Macmillan, pp. 1–22.

Levitt, P. and Glick Schiller, N. (2004) Conceptualizing Simultaneity: A Transnational Social Field Perspective on Society, *International Migration Review*, 38 (3), 1002–1039.

Lowell, B. L. and Findlay, A. (2001) *Migration of Highly Skilled Persons from Developing Countries: Impact and Policy Responses.* Synthesis report. International Migration Paper, 44. Geneva: International Labour Office.

Mai, N. and Paladini, C. (2013) Flexible Circularities: Integration, Return and Socio-Economic Instability within the Albanian Migration to Italy. In: Triandafyllidou, A. (ed.) *Circular Migration Between Europe and its Neighbourhood.* Oxford: Oxford University Press, pp. 42–68.

Maroukis, T. and Gemi, E. (2013) Circular Migration between Greece and Albania: Beyond the State? In: Triandafyllidou A. (ed.) *Circular Migration between Europe and its Neighbourhood: Choice or Necessity.* Oxford: Oxford University Press, pp. 68–89.

Mema, D., Aliaj, S., and Matoshi, A. (2019) *Beyond Borders: Analytical Research Report on Migration in Albania.* Tirane: Mary Ward Loreto Foundation.

MoIA (2015) *Albania Extended Migration Profile 2012–2014.* Tirana: Ministry of Internal Affairs and IOM.

Morokvasic, M. (2003) Transnational Mobility and Gender: A View from Postwall Europe. In: Morokvasic, M., Erel, U., and Shinozaki, K. (eds) *Crossing Borders and Shifting Boundaries.* Berlin: Springer, pp. 101–136.

Morokvasic, M. (2014) Gendering Migration. *Migracijske i etničke teme*, 30 (3), 355–378.

Nadler, R., Lang, T., Glorius, B., and Kovács, Z. (2016) Conclusions: Current and Future Perspectives on Return Migration and Regional Development in Europe. In: Nadler, R., Kovács, Z., Glorius, B., and Lang, T. (eds) *Return Migration and Regional Development in Europe. Mobility Against the Stream.* Basingstoke: Palgrave Macmillan, pp. 291–376.

Pojani, D. (2010) City Profile: Tirana. *Cities*, 27 (6), 483–495.

Porobic, S. (2017) 'Invisible' Returns of Bosnian Refugees and Their Psychosocial Wellbeing. In: Vathi, Z. and King, R. (eds) *Return Migration and Psychosocial Wellbeing: Discourses, Policymaking and Outcomes for Migrants and their Families.* Abingdon: Routledge, pp. 108–125.

Reiner, M. and Dragos, R. (2012) Return Migration: The Experience of Eastern Europe. *International Migration*, 50 (6), 109–128.

RoA (2017) The National Strategy on Diaspora and Migration 2018–2024. Available at: http://diaspora.gov.al/wp-content/uploads/2017/12/Strategy-English.pdf [Accessed 8 September 2020].

Thilo, L., Glorius, B., Nadler, R., and Kovács, Z. (2016) Introduction: Mobility Against the Stream? New Concepts, Methodological Approaches and Regional Perspectives on Return Migration in Europe. In: Nadler, R., Kovács, Z., Glorius, B., and Lang, T. (eds) *Return Migration and Regional Development in Europe. Mobility Against the Stream.* Basingstoke: Palgrave Macmillan, pp. 1–22.

Vathi, Z. (2017) The Interface between Return Migration and Psychosocial Wellbeing. In: Vathi, Z. and Kind, R. (eds) *Return Migration and Psychosocial Wellbeing Discourses, Policy-Making and Outcomes for Migrants and their Families.* Abingdon: Routledge, pp. 1–18.

Vathi, Z and Zajmi, I. (2017) *Children and Migration in Albania: Latest Trends and Protection Measures Available.* Tirane: Terre des hommes in Albania.

Vullnetari, J. (2015) Albanian Seasonal Work Migration to Greece: A Case of Last Resort? In: Vermeulen, H., Baldwin-Edwards, M., and van Boeschoten, R. (eds) *Migration in the Southern Balkans From Ottoman Territory to Globalized Nation States.* IMISCOE Research Series. Berlin: Springer, pp. 143–159.

World Bank (2015) *Country Partnership Framework for Albania 2015–2019.* Washington DC: World Bank. Available at: www.worldbank.org/en/country/albania/publication/albania-country-partnership-framework-2015#:~:text=The%20World%20Bank%20Group's%20new%20Country%20Partnership%20Framework%20for%20Albania,public%20services%20for%20its%20citizens [Accessed 8 September 2020].

4 Return mobilities of the second generation
Between disintegration and hybrid identities

Introduction

Whilst there is considerable academic work on integration, circular, and transnational mobility of Albanians in Greece and Italy (indicatively, Maroukis and Gemi 2013; Gemi 2016; Vathi 2015; Mai 2011; Mai and Paladini 2013; Paladini 2014), there is a gap in research on actual return migration and mobility of second-generation migrants. In fact, the study of returnees of second generation in the country of origin (Albania) and embarking on an intergenerational comparative approach has been an underexplored field of Albanian migration research, more generally. It should be acknowledged, however, that this is a relatively new phenomenon and field of study given the recent (historical time) apocalyptic exodus of Albanians in the early1990s.

Chapter 3 explored the dynamic nature of return and remigration of first-generation Albanian migrant returnees from Greece and Italy. We have shown how relocating back to the home country has at times been coupled with seasonal or circular migration between the origin and destination countries. Transnational connections and mobility have been integral part of the return experience of first-generation migrants going back to Albania.

This chapter turns to the experiences of return and mobility among young, second-generation 'returnees'. Our analysis focuses on 16 young Albanian men and women who were born and raised in Italy or Greece and who relocated to Albania as teenagers or young adults, usually together with their parents. Indeed, strictly speaking these interviewees are not returnees as they were born in the destination countries. Our analysis in fact points to their return journey narratives, their (re)integration challenges, and post-return experiences as it seeks to map out the mobility patterns (internal and international) before and after the return to Albania.

84 Return mobilities of the second generation

There is special focus on their integration experiences in Greece and Italy, without neglecting the impact of economic crisis in shaping their social space alongside their legal status/citizenship that enables them to navigate the uncharted waters of mobility and negotiate their journey of return or onward mobility or both. More concretely, the chapter delves into the topic of 'micro-internalities' (pre- and post-return individual experiences) as well as the 'macro-externalities' (collective and socio-economic effects) that shed light on how the personal plan of action is constructed and contextualized (King and Kılınc 2014: 127).

Setting the context of second-generation (dis)integration, return, and mobility

Most of the literature on the children of migrants born in Europe or the USA argues that the economic, social, and political lives of second-generation individuals differ from both those of their peers with no migratory background and hose of their migrant parents (Chimienti et al. 2019:1). In fact, these individuals are not migrants, although the term 'second-generation migrant' is commonly used. The young people interviewed in this study were born in the destination country or moved there at pre-school age, with little if any memories of their parents' homeland. They have gone through the Greek and Italian school systems, developed social identities rooted in references to the mainstream population and its institutions, mastered the Greek or Italian language, and often form very solid relationships with native peers.

This study adopts an expanded definition of 'second generation' that includes both those children born in Greece or Italy to Albanian parents (first-generation migrants) and those children who were born in Albania but migrated to the host country at an early age. Let us however delve a little deeper into considering how 'early age' is defined in the relevant literature and what kind of implications it has with regard to those second-generation young migrants returning to their parental homeland.

Different studies adopt diverging cut-off points as to who should be considered a first- and second-generation migrant. Child (1943), Portes and Zhou (1993), and Louie (2006) include in their definition of 'second generation' children born abroad who migrated to the United States before the age of 12 and who were educated and socialized in the United States. In European studies of the second generation, Andall (2002) in her study of African Italians in Italy defines the second generation as those born in Italy or who arrived before the age of six. In similar vein, Crul and Vermuelen (2003) converge with Andall in defining the second generation as those children who were born in the destination country or who arrived there before starting elementary school (Andall 2002: 971).

However, other scholars have argued for a more nuanced definition that highlights the complexity and ambivalence of this dual belonging of children who migrated to a foreign country at an early age. They thus offer a classification of the second generation as those born at destination, and then speak of the 1.75, 1.5, and 1.25 generations by referring respectively to foreign-born children arriving before the age of six, those arriving between six and 12 years of age, and finally those arriving in their teens, i.e. from the ages of 12 to 17 (Rumbaut 1997). Regarding the latter, the scope is to distinguish between the unique socialization experience of those who were not born at destination but also were not adults when they moved. These intermediate generations are distinct from those who arrived as adults as they mainly acquired their socialization through the school system instead of the workplace (Rumbaut 2004; Da Cruz 2018: 42). Finally, in an attempt to create a more conceptually oriented category of second generation (instead of a numerical one), some scholars offer a simple categorical definition, namely 'post-immigrant generation' (Rumbaut 2004) or 'post-migrant generation' (Wessendorf 2007).

As the key term in defining the generational boundaries of the migrant population in the host country has been the process of socialization, a central issue to all approaches is the question of integration (or assimilation) of the second generation, their progressive loss of ethnic distinctiveness (King and Christou 2008: 6), and their socio-economic mobility (upwards or not) as compared with that of their peers with non-migrant parents.

Two major theories have influenced the analysis of the second-generation integration process. First, the linear assimilation theory (Gordon 1964) which suggested a straightforward upward mobility in education and the labour market. The assimilationist perspective explained integration through the lens of migrants' characteristics, including cultural explanations, without paying sufficient attention to the structural and institutional barriers such as legal status, limited access to citizenship and education, discrimination, and lack of political recognition (Chimienti et al. 2019: 4). Two decades later, this model was subject to criticism by Portes and Zou (1993), who emphasized the role of structural determinants in shaping the outcome of the integration process. They proposed the now well-known concept of 'segmented assimilation'. According to their theory, the second generation may experience classical assimilation, downward mobility, or a combination of upward mobility with biculturalism (Portes and Rumbaut 2001; Portes and

Zhou 1993). In response to this approach of Portes and co-authors, Alba and Nee (2003) reconsidered the linear assimilationist theory, still arguing that (linear) assimilation will blur the structural differences and eventually both first and second generations are likely to experience upward mobility. For Portes, however, the embedded social stratification (non-white racial status) along with economic instability will hamper both first and second generations' upward mobility. Seeking to compensate for the structural barriers experienced, migrants will turn their attention to their own community, asking for support and solidarity in their pathway to integration. Meanwhile, this kind of mobility has been commonly identified with downward assimilation or the negative role of community on mobility (Thomson and Crul 2007: 1036; Chimienti et al. 2019: 4) even though this approach is not eventually fully corroborated by relevant research in both the USA and Europe (Boyd 2002; Farley and Alba 2002; Hirschman 2001; Waldinger 2007; Waldinger and Feliciano 2004).

Contemporary theoretical approaches have paid more attention to political and institutional factors affecting integration for both the first- and the expanded second-generation migrants. The 'citizenship approach' (Brubaker 1992; Castles and Miller 2003; Joppke 1999) explains different integration outcomes as a function of different national citizenship models/policies of integration. And in turn these different national citizenship models and approaches to integration are shaped by the wider welfare system and migration policies of each country (Schierup, Hansen, and Castles 2006). Crul and Vermeulen (2003) by contrast, emphasize the role of institutional arrangements, in general, as offering better explanations than distinct national models for the variation in integration patterns of the second generation across Europe. The 'institutional approach' finds the explanation of differences observed in integration trajectories of the second generation in the societal context rather than in migrants and specific integration policies *per se*.

More recent studies have moved beyond conventional (meso or macro) approaches by extending their focus on feelings of belonging and identity construction. They have pointed to the multifaceted, situational, hybrid, and complex sense of identity that second-generation migrants develop (Malson et al. 2002; Frisina 2007; Sansone 1995). Anthropologists have also criticized the above classical models of integration which see the second (and/or third) generation either following the straight line towards complete assimilation to the mainstream culture or remaining 'locked' in their parents' culture and tradition (Berthoud 2000; Elliot 2009: 2). In contrast to 'segmented assimilation' theory mentioned above, the concept of a 'third space' (Bhabha 1990) probing to an alternative space where new hybrid cultural forms emerge at the intersection of different cultures has taken higher prominence, particularly when it comes to second-generation return or onward migration.

In Europe, the debate on the second generation became popular with regard to their precarious socio-economic situation and their presumed lack of integration (or assimilation). The concept was first used in the 1970s when the category 'second generation' and the term 'integration' highlighted both the colonial and assimilationist perspectives towards the individuals of migratory background born on European soil (Wihtol de Wenden 2005). This was particularly the case in countries where the principle of *ius sanguinis* prevailed and access to citizenship was not automatic even for those born in the country, such as for instance in Switzerland, Germany, or Austria but also in our two destination countries of concern here, notably Italy and Greece. This does not mean that second-generation migrants did not encounter important barriers to socio-economic integration and upward mobility in countries like France or the UK where a *ius soli* citizenship definition prevailed (Chimienti et al. 2019: 3). In contrast to previous decades, the 2000s marked the beginning of a different trajectory where second generations experienced a 'disillusionment' towards the host country identity because of the lack of political recognition and representation as well as ongoing discrimination (Wihtol de Wenden 2005). This, in turn, led to different kind of transnational ties and links via differing attachments with their parents' homeland, including the likelihood of 'return' to the parental country of origin (Thurairajah 2017: 116; Chimienti et al. 2019: 3). Indeed, until recently, there was little or no expectation that the second generation of migratory background would return to their parents' homeland, although there is a growing, and distinctive, literature on second-generation or counter-diasporic return migration (Wessendorf 2007; King and Christou 2008; Sardinha 2011; Teerling 2011).

Indeed, there is a great deal of doubt as to whether the process of voluntary relocation or going back to their parents' homeland or birthplace can be considered return migration. While the term 'return' is traditionally used to illustrate the resettlement of the first generation in their homeland, it sounds quite problematic to use it for the second generation since they decide to move to or settle in a country which is probably not seen as 'home' as they were not born and raised there (King and Kılınc 2016: 168). This blurred image or feeling about 'home' can be best explained by what Jean-Pierre Cassarino (2004) sees as the second generation's specific situation, where return is viewed as an episode in their migration mobilities, including their transnational family ties to the country of origin. If these ties are strong, return is more likely to happen. Otherwise, if there is no special social and emotional attachment to their parents' home country, return is much less likely to occur (Kılınc 2014: 8). However, in the context of transnationalism, we can better conceptualize the dynamics of return in relation to how both countries (host and origin) affect the evolution of second-generation identities (Portes et al. 1999: 219) and, of course, their socio-economic upward mobility.

In the context of the Albanian second generation in Greece and Italy, Vathi (2011, 2015) has compared the attitudes to return of Albanian first- and second-generation migrants in Greece, Italy, and the UK, focusing in particular on the interface between return migration and psychosocial wellbeing (see Vathi and King 2017 and also Cela 2017) or in the realm of social protection and access to welfare of return migrants from Greece to Albania (Vathi et al. 2019).

Recent research has studied diasporic youth identities of second-generation Albanian migrants involved in transnational mobility during the recent economic crisis (Michail and Christou 2016, 2018), looking at the various dimensions of their mobility and agency. Other studies have also investigated the reintegration process for children of returnee emigrants in the Albanian educational system (Vathi et al. 2016; Hoxha-Laro 2012). In terms of 'mobilities', research by Karamoschou (2018) and King and Karamoschou (2019) sheds light on the new phenomenon of onward migration of Albanian second-generation migrants fleeing Greece's fragmented socio-economic reality to the UK. When it comes to 'return mobilities' (King 2011), it should be underlined that in contrast to the first generation, the second generation has a different understanding of home and different perception of identity and sense of belonging. Their upbringing and patterns of socialization as both Greek/Italian and EU citizens in connection with transnational links to Albania have created a hybrid construction of identity, belonging, and home.

The experiences narrated by our respondents can offer a powerful introductory note to the real-life stories of the children of Albanian migrants in Greece and Italy. What is more, they can best illustrate the fundamental differences between the socialization patterns and identity formation of the second generation in contrast to their parents.

> I remember myself, two years old in Chalkida [a small city north of Athens] in my mom's work. I used to go with her since I was two years old. While my mom was cleaning, the landlady took

care of me. I always played with her. But then my mom quit the job at this lady ... Then I remember my brother. He was four and I was two years old and he was taking care of me. That is, my mom left us for eight hours alone. Without uncles, without aunts.

(GR-01)

Stress, fatigue from the hard work, I was also a little naughty child. I made a fuss at home and my mother when back at home, tired from the hard work, should pick up my mess. I saw my parents very tired, all the time. My father was a classic Albanian, he came home from work, took the remote control in hand, drank beers and watched TV.

(GR-10)

I had difficulty in making friends. I did not go out at all. My life was, home, school, and lessons. I also did some housework as my mother was more in Albania than in Italy.

(IT-05)

(Dis)integration, stigmatization, and 'disguised' identities

While Chapter 3 showed how the economic crisis in Greece and Italy and the resulting unemployment or underemployment of Albanian migrants was a decisive factor pushing them to return to Albania, what emerges from the narratives of our second-generation interviewees is the importance of citizenship and an overall feeling of socio-political belonging – or, in their case, stigmatization and exclusion – experienced at the destination country, even when they were born there. These parameters of socio-political integration were an important element that together with socio-economic difficulties shaped the second generation's attitudes towards staying or returning. Our study revealed several alternative scenarios of staying/deeper integration in the host country: return and relocation to their parents' homeland or a more fluid transnational or circulatory mobility between the two or opting for onward migration elsewhere, as Zana Vathi (2011) had also outlined.

Without exception, respondents' narratives revolved around legal and structural exclusion, stigmatization in their daily life, and the economic crisis as the main sources of disintegration and 'disguised' identities. They especially refer to the labyrinthine bureaucratic regulations in force in Italy and Greece (King and Mai 2004) for their parents to obtain and renew stay permits (*avere I documenti*/εξασφάλιση χαρτιών) and, of course, the extremely problematic legal status of the second generation who did not have a secure legal status at the age of majority (Andall 2002; Frisina 2007). This insecurity was a palpable element of their immigration experience since childhood:

> My father left for Italy in 1995, a friend helped him to cross the sea as he transported clandestine migrants in from Durres to Italy. Afterward he got papers, rent his own house and after six years we went too. To enter Italy, we used the papers of our relatives who happened to have the same age with us. My father could not get paper for family reunification as he did not meet the requirements, initially. When I arrived there, my aunt, who worked in a school, helped me to enrol in the first grade and this helped me, my mother and my sister to apply for resident permits.
>
> (IT-04)

For young second-generation individuals, the question of having or not having documents, citizenship, or a permanent residence permit is not only an annoying and frustrating burden with important practical and material consequences but also has the power to instil in them a sense of the marginalized 'other'. Lenci migrated to Italy at the age of seven after a clandestine crossing of the Adriatic Sea (in 1997) to join his father who had previously migrated to Italy and settled in a small city of Piedmont, in northern Italy. In 2015, after 18 years of living, schooling, and working in Italy, he was 'forced' to return to his parents' home in Shkodra and become a circular/seasonal migrant.

> We had never thought to return to Albania. My parents' plan was to live in Italy. The lifestyle there was better and there were job opportunities as well. But in the meantime, my father died and I do not have permanent stay permit or citizenship ... I use to return back to Italy since there in summer started the working season of collecting fruit. I work there from August 'til November and then come back to Shkodra where I work in a 'call centre'.
>
> (IT-06)

The main implication of similar stories of those interviewees born or born and raised in host countries is that they do not (legally) belong to the country (Andall 2002: 394). For most of the respondents, turning 18 was a kind of culture shock, as they unexpectedly found themselves to have no legal ties to the host country as they were no longer legally linked to their parents and had to apply for a separate residence permit (for work or study) while access to naturalization was (at least until 2015) a 'summer night's dream'.

> Since I turned 17, I submitted the papers for Greek citizenship. They were frozen for three years and I finally got my citizenship this summer [2016], after insisting many times for re- evaluation of my file. My brother was not so lucky even though he was born in Greece. They do not give him citizenship because he needed a paper that he is still a student at the time of application. My dad has the 'ten-year' resident permit and my mom the 'five-year' resident permit. My brother has no papers at all.
>
> (GR-04).

It is widely recognized that access to citizenship is a key variable in assessing integration and migration policies. Despite the change in both countries' demographic composition since the 1990s, the citizenship regime in both Italy and Greece has remained largely based on *ius sanguinis*. In the best of cases, naturalization is conceptualized as a 'reward' (Jurado 2008: 5) for migrant assimilation rather than as an institutional tool for deeper and substantial integration (Gemi 2019: 120). Importantly, citizenship is defined in ethnic-genealogical and cultural terms with little reference to civic elements and the possibility to 'become' rather than 'be born' Greek (Triandafyllidou et al. 2015).

> I'm 18 years old and I haven't yet got the Greek citizenship. I was born in Albania. My parents migrated to Greece when I was 28 days old.
>
> (GR-01)

Indeed, five out of six respondents returning from Italy hold some sort of temporary or indefinite residence permit, while the sixth does not have one.

> After turning 18 it was difficult to take citizenship so every year I renewed the residence permit 'til I returned to Albania and lost it.
>
> (IT-01)

Italian citizenship law prioritizes *ius sanguinis* over *ius soli*, making access to citizenship for the second generation a complex process, particularly for those without an EU passport. The law does not recognize the children of two foreign parents as Italian nationals until their eighteenth birthday, when they have one year to request citizenship, and requires that applicants demonstrate uninterrupted residence in the country since birth (Zincone and Basili 2009). Thus, children born to foreign parents in Italy could be socially and culturally integrated, yet they lack the citizenship that would guarantee equality of rights, freedoms, and mobility (Clough Marinaro and Walston 2010: 8).

In contrast to Italy, half of respondents (five out of ten) returning from Greece already have or are in the process of acquiring Greek citizenship; one holds a second-generation residence permit and four do not possess any documents that would give them status in Greece. Without exception, respondents holding Greek passports acquired them in 2016–2017, clearly as a result of citizenship law reforms (Law 4332/19.07.2015), which facilitated the acquisition of Greek citizenship by second-generation migrants. It is worth noting that Greek citizenship law had been reformed already in 2010; Law 3838/2010 gave citizenship at birth to children of foreign parents born in Greece who resided in Greece and had attended Greek public schools. However, that law was declared unconstitutional in 2013 by a Supreme Court decision on grounds that formal requisites could not suffice for attributing citizenship. The court introduced a distinction between those of 'Greek soil/origin' and others, arguing that the first should have priority over others in terms of citizenship (Iliadis 2014: 6). The reform was taken up again in 2015 by the then-newly elected left-wing government which introduced Law 4332/2015 making naturalization possible with a simple declaration/application for children born in Greece and for youth who have completed most of their education in Greece.

> Now I have the Greek passport, I got it in 2016. My dad holds a long-term residence permit. He has been trying to get citizenship for six years.
>
> (GR-06)

In a study of the educational and labour market trajectories of second-generation youth (Cavounidis and Cholezas 2013), citizenship was found to be a crucial factor differentiating the labour market and marriage strategies that they developed. In fact, given that second-generation Albanian migrants cannot acquire a residence permit through their parents after the age of 18 and must acquire an independent permit by virtue of employment with social insurance contributions or study at a public institution, they have often adopted various strategies for securing legal status, notably through marriage to a Greek citizen or to a holder of a co-ethnic residence permit (κάρτα ομογενούς) so as to secure a permit for 'family reunification' purposes as a spouse (Cavounidis 2018: 22–23).

Both the Greek and Italian models of migration governance have a direct impact on the second generation's sense of identity and belonging:

> I always had the impression that in Greece I would just remain a migrant with a university degree. It has to do with the fact that you will never have same treatment with a Greek.
>
> (GR-04).

Almost all respondents had a story to tell about cumbersome legal requirements and experiences of discrimination as the main obstacles against feeling accepted and equal citizens of host countries. The feelings of belonging and stigmatization were often intertwined as one respondent explained: he was accepted because he did not 'look exactly as an Albanian' even though he 'had a different name' (compared to his Italian origin classmates):

> at school I began to realize that I was not Italian. I had a different name but this did not make any difference in relations with my peers. Indeed I have always been told that I do not look exactly as an Albanian.
>
> (IT-01)

In terms of integration in the educational system, some respondents in Greece highlighted how frustrating and enraging it was to have to deal with teachers' overwhelming assimilationist and discriminatory classroom practices.

> They tried to change my name from Doris to Theodora but I always insisted to call me with my birth name Doris...All the time that I wrote the name Doris in my notebook the teacher deleted it and wrote instead Theodora. This pissed me off a lot.
>
> (GR-03)

In contrast to Greece, the experience of integration in Italian school was positive for Anxhi:

> I did not know the language, other than some words I heard from my cousins. But in Italian schools there is provision for supplementary teaching for foreign students to learn the language. So, after the regular classes I sat with a specific teacher for 2–3 hours who helped me with my language and lessons.
>
> (IT-04)

What clearly emerged from fieldwork, in fact, was the profound impact of host countries' public discourse on respondents' everyday lives, their identity formation, and their sense of belonging.

> A child every time he disagreed with me, he said to me 'you shut up your mouth because you are Albanian' or 'that you are animals'. Some also kept asking me questions like 'do you have potatoes or tomatoes in Albania'. Such questions were asked not only by my classmates but also by adult people in the neighbourhood where we lived. This makes you feel a little strange, it made it difficult for me to adapt ... I always feel like a foreigner in Greece. When I go to Albania, I am a foreigner again. Now that I go to Greece, I see it as a vacation. I no longer see it as my place.
>
> (GR- 03)

In particular, racist comments from peers and discriminatory attitudes both emerged as having the effect of stigmatization and marginalization.

> I remember this episode ... it stuck in my mind. I can't forget it. It was a little girl playing ball with other children. I approached them and I told them that I wanted to join them. This little girl replied to me that 'my dad does not let me play with you'. I just started crying. I was also a 7- [or] 8-year-old girl.
>
> (GR-06)

> I have experienced racism a little less than my brother. My brother was a very good student. He was to carry the flag [at the national celebration parade]. They did not allow him to carry the flag just because he was Albanian. They gave it to a girl who had lower grades than my brother just because she was Greek ... My brother kept telling me 'I want to be a doctor'. His classmates made fun of him by telling him 'you doctor (!!), you are a little Albanian'. Albanians will remain workers, always workers, and they will be only depended workers on a day-wage (μεροκάματο) ... When he was told that he would carry the flag, some children threw

> sandwiches at him. I was there witnessing what happened. Then I went to the one who threw the sandwich and I told him don't dare to touch my brother ... and he pushed me away. Then my brother came and pushed him back and he was punished by the school director.
>
> (GR-01)

Discrimination is amplified by the mainstream media's implicit linking of criminality and Albanians. This process stigmatized not only first- but also second-generation Albanians, who were raised in a toxic environment, reproducing the negative image of Albanians as thieves and criminals. A 2011 study of three Greek newspapers of varying political orientation found that one in four articles about Albanians concerned criminality and deviant behaviour (Tsaliki 2011). The dominant negative portrayal of Albanians brought as an outcome the internalization of stigma by the second-generation Albanians.

In their attempt to integrate and be de-stigmatized, the majority of second-generation Albanians were forced to hide their identity, highlight their 'Greekness', and disassociate themselves from people who represented the stereotypical image of Albanians in Greece. Practices adopted as part of Albanian migrants' efforts to remain 'invisible' in Greece (Kokkali 2011) included changing their names and being baptized Orthodox. This supports the argument of adjustment strategy developed by second-generation Albanians as a response to the assimilationist pressures of Greek society.

> In passport my name is Anjeza but I had been baptized as Maria. My brother was baptized Giannis. We changed also our family name from Hysa to Pacolli.
>
> (GR-05)

> My dad's Albanian name is Hysen and he changed it to Ilias. And my mom from Aurela made it Rena. That's how they were called.
>
> (GR-06)

There are also language shift tendencies among the second generation of Albanians in Greece (Gogonas 2010; Michail 2010; Chatzidaki and Xenikaki 2012), with many rarely speaking any Albanian in public. This suggests a tendency among Albanians to self-assimilate, which in turn is viewed as a 'mimesis' (Paladini 2014) and conformity with the existing system of cultural values of Greek society. Our study also corroborates this by pinpointing an inclination on the part of the second generation to feel more integrated in Greece while maintaining their preference for using Greek across all communicative activities.

> The first three years were difficult until the children got used to me. I think in trying to get closer to them I forgot about Albania and Albanian language. But a child in order to belong somewhere and feel accepted does everything possible.
>
> (GR-06)

Indeed, the majority of second-generation Albanian migrants attends Greek schools that lack 'intercultural' spirit (Chatzidaki and Maligkoudi 2012). Importantly enough, while knowledge of Greek for the first generation constitutes a practical necessity and a vehicle of social mobility, for the second generation, Greek is the main language in which they became socialized and therefore constitutes a core element for their identity construction process.

> I am more identified with Greece. It is easier for me to speak Greek, to think Greek, everything. I had a teacher who told me that when you manage to think in Albanian then you consider yourself Albanian.
>
> (GR-06)

Some studies (Gogonas 2010; Michail 2010) found that a basic reason leading second-generation Albanian migrants to conceal their ethnic language is the stigmatization and lack of institutional support from both Albania and host countries for teaching Albanian in Greek and Italian schools. Other studies show that Greek teachers treat second-generation bilingualism as an obstacle more than as an asset (Gkaintartzi et al. 2014). At the same time, Albanian parents do not engage in systematic efforts to support Albanian language maintenance (Chatzidaki and Maligkoudi 2012), while participation in Albanian language classes organized by the various Albanian communities is very low (Gogonas and Michail 2014).

In Italy, research has shown that educational achievements of second-generation high school students are generally lower than their Italian peers (Casacchia 2007). Evidently, keeping up with the academic performance of their Italian schoolmates is a major problem faced by second-generation students (Elliot 2009: 7). Albanian children who migrated to Italy at a young age often have to repeat early schooling.

One of the biggest difficulties was the refusal to recognize some school years I did in Albania as the two countries have different education systems. So I started from the beginning.

(IT-05)

In a study of Albanian primary school pupils in the south of Italy, Zinn (2005) emphasizes how 'Italian schools appear widely off the mark in terms of striving to reach the intercultural pedagogic ideal of considering diversity a resource' (ibid.: 263). This attitude impacts second-generation Albanians' sense of belonging and identity as it tends to accentuate their 'difference' from their schoolmates. In some cases, discriminatory attitudes had profound effects on their academic and even individual trajectories. King and Mai (2004) support that stereotypical representations of Albanian migrants have a direct impact on their life trajectories by becoming 'powerful agents of discrimination infiltrating every aspect of social interactions' (ibid.: 471).

As the economic crisis in Greece resulted in a large number of Albanian immigrants embarking on a return journey to Albania (Maroukis 2012; Michail 2013), knowledge of Albanian became important and necessary for the second generation. As elaborated below, the recent return trend is accompanied by more positive attitudes to the Albanian language. Furthermore, it exerts a significant impact on how the identities of young returnee Albanians are constructed and negotiated in their parents' homeland (Gogonas and Michail 2014: 12).

With regards to mobility, recent studies (Gemi 2019; King and Karamoschou 2019) have shown that even in a situation of crisis, rather than going back to Albania or staying in Greece, second-generation Albanians have recently embarked on an onward migration journey to other Western countries they consider more advanced (ibid.: 109). Even a decade ago, studies of second-generation Albanians in Greece and Italy (Athanasopoulou 2007; Zinn 2005) found that they were planning to leave Greece and Italy due to the legal and social exclusion and vulnerability they felt.

Engaging in new forms of mobility has provoked the phenomenon of disintegration, and immigrants are severing connections that once tied them to Greece and Italy. The economic crisis triggered an evaluation of resources and networks in both host and origin countries. As shown above, second-generation Albanians reconsidered their livelihoods and are contemplating emigration once more: back to their origin country or to another country. As Koopmans et al. (2005) note, the strong transnational orientation may be a response to exclusionary citizenship regimes in host states that limit migrants' access to the political community (ibid.: 142). In fact, when transnationalism emanates from exclusion in the host society there is a negative integration denominator (Bivand Erdal and Oeppen 2013: 878). For second-generation Albanians the economic crisis and the difficulties in acquiring Greek citizenship become strong push factors for re-migration either to another European country or overseas (Michail and Christou 2016: 8).

> The only thing I miss are my [Greek] friends. Nothing connects me with Greece anymore. Even my friendships have gone to Italy, England, or other cities in Greece. So there is nothing left in Crete.
> (GR-04)

Trajectories of return 'mobilities'

One could say that for second-generation Albanians in Greece and Italy, true return might be interpreted just as easily as a movement back and forth from Greece and Italy to their parents' or wider family's home in Albania.

> I really liked Albania. Five months after my birth in Greece my mother brought me to Albania and I stayed with my grandmother for almost two years. My dad worked as a baker and my parents had no one to look after me. I remember my five-year-old sister taking care of me at first, and then my sister's [Greek] god mother taking me to her house to feed me as I cried. So under these difficult circumstances my parents decided to send me to my grandmother in Albania. I lived in Albania until I was two years old. After I turned eight, I used to visit Albania every year during the summer.
> (GR-02)

Visiting home by the younger second generation can have various outcomes. Depending on circumstances, such trips may end up in recalling beautiful memories and create a deeper attachment to and identification with the home of their parents and grandparents.

> I used to visit to Albania regularly since we got the papers [2001]. We visit it every summer, from mid-July to the end of August.

> I felt perfect. I was excited about the fact that I was changing environment, that I was meeting my grandparents.
>
> (GR-10)

> I used to visit Albania very rarely. The last few years that I visited it often I started to like it very much. I start feeling love for my 'place' and 'home'.
>
> (GR-08)

However, these visits can have the opposite outcome, namely reinforcing their sense of how 'Greek' and 'Italian' they are and convince them that their parents' home country can never become their home (Kibria 2002).

> We visited Albania regularly. My mom liked to go there every weekend as we were close (half an hour). So we used to visit my grandpa's house. But then I started speaking (only) Greek and I could not communicate with my grandparents. I did not like Albania. I did not want to go there.
>
> (GR-06)

In any case, attachment to the homeland is a key constituent of 'diasporic consciousness' (Vertovec 1997), which according to Clifford (1994) 'makes the best of a bad situation' caused by the experience of loss and marginality. It is often reinforced by, among other things, blocked advancement (ibid.: 312) transmitted across generations by memories of a collective past. It is argued that this type of diaspora consciousness is generated among contemporary transnational communities who acknowledge their multi-locality and the necessity of interconnection that goes beyond the real or imagined national borders (Vertovec 1997; King and Kılınc 2014). To this end, memory plays a key and highly complex role in the construction of the diaspora's consciousness and the maintenance of diasporic identities generated by nuclear and extended family.

> I visited Albania every summer. We have a house over here, in the city of Lac. We used to gather with the cousins. We took the bus and enjoy the whole route to the village. The small river. The trees. The donkeys. The pigs. Grandma was always waiting for us at the bus station. I still miss that hug.
>
> (GR-01)

Most of the Albanians of second generation who return to their parents' country of origin exhibit complex articulations and experiences of home and belonging. Several are more grounded in where 'home' is and where they truly belong.

> I grew up in Greece with the Greek mentality. I feel like that there is my home.
>
> (GR-09)

> I wanted to stay in Greece. To study, to make my life there. When you are born in Greece, when you grow up there and when your family is there, it is difficult to come to Albania. And my parents wanted that too, to sit and stay in Greece.
>
> (GR-06)

Most of our respondents display a clear and rational attitude of their (dual) identity while rejecting the cliché that second generations are somehow suspended between two or more cultural worlds in a limbo of conflicting identities and role models. The following passage illustrates the experience of Arbi (who returned with his family as a teenager) in confronting others' stereotypes about his origin:

> In [secondary] school people kept asking me 'where you are from' and they were waiting for me to name a Greek city. I told them 'I am from Albania'. I did not want to hide my origin as sooner or later the truth will come forth. At first they may have doubt believing that I might be such a person as those showed on TV, but as they got to know me they realized that I was not that kind of person so we came very close.
>
> (GR-02)

Vathi (2009), in her analysis of intergenerational transmission between first- and second-generation Albanians in Tuscany, highlighted the role of the legal context in which parents migrated to Italy and how their own experiences of integration affected the processes of communication and exchange of cultural values with their children.

> I was raised with the idea that I must learn my mother tongue and love who I am. My parents also disagreed with the behaviour of many Albanians in Greece. However, they never hid their origin, as many Albanians did, saying that they were from Northern

Epirus [meaning they are Albanians of Greek ethnic origin]. My father was authentic and a proud man.

(GR-10)

As we argued also in Chapter 2, returning to Albania in the 2000s was considered an act of failure. This trend, however, changes in the 2010s for both the first and second generations as they developed new forms of connections with both the origin and destination countries, living somehow 'in between'. This was certainly linked to strategies of socio-economic resilience through circular migration rather than return, as the onset of the economic crisis, particularly in Greece, pushed many families to return to Albania while circulating between the two countries for work:

> My parents return to Greece every year because they work there over the summers. My parents are circular. They come and go. In winter you'll find them in Albania and in summer in Greece. My father leaves in March and my mother later in June and they both return in October. They work together in the same company, regularly. I only go there on vacation, for just a month. What you can earn in Greece for a month, you get in Albania for six months.
>
> (GR-04)

This pattern was also adopted by second-generation youth who returned to Greece during the summer season to work in the tourism and catering industry:

> Since I was 15, I have been working in the summers in Greece. I started as a waiter in a hotel and then in a cafeteria. Every summer I go to Greece and work in a bar.
>
> (GR- 07)

Another dimension of return, usually ignored, is multiple return visits, which as Vathi (2015: 124) maintains, have changed in terms of their meaning and frequency over time. In some cases, this might reflect the trend of downward mobility or is a part of return scenarios' preparedness.

> When we migrated to Greece we always had the idea that in a few years we will return to Albania ... my parents returned to Albania three months after me. They saw my return as their opportunity

> to return. They realized that things in Greece were getting worse, the rent was high, the living cost was also high and the income was low. My father no longer had a permanent job as an electrician. Working only during the summer was not enough to make ends meet.
>
> (GR-04)

> [M]y parents enrolled my sister to a school in Albania, Arsakeio, to get a recognized diploma. So, my sister had already returned to Albania and that was the reason for us to return. In addition, my parents wanted to return to their homeland. I didn't take it badly.
>
> (GR-02)

Our second-generation informants also confirm the importance of previous investments made by the household in real estate, such as having bought a house or also a shop through which they could make some income

> Since 1999 we bought our house. It was a common decision to get a house in Tirana as soon as we got the opportunity, a house in a good place and at a good price. Initially I stayed at my aunt's until my parents returned and then we moved into our own house.
>
> (GR-04)

> We bought a house in Elbasan. My parents always had in mind that one day we will return to Albania so we would need our own house.
>
> (GR 09)

For those who had not managed to invest in Albania, their return depended on the resources of family networks in Albania as a survival strategy plan.

> We returned to Elbasan, to my grandparents' house. After realizing the situation, I moved to Tirana together with my mother. We rented a house. I had a cousin of mine who had a restaurant and had a job, I went there and they all helped me a lot.
>
> (IT-01)

Some parents saw their investments during the migration years as a provision for housing and employment, for them and their children, in case of return. But, in many cases, in our study and likewise in Vathi's work (Vathi 2015: 134), the issue of return was resisted by the children because they felt alien towards Albania while they identified with the lifestyle of the host countries. In the frame of family decision of return, our respondents returned to Albania when they were teenagers, either still in elementary or secondary school or at the end of the academic year.

> I have always disagreed with the idea of return. I did not want to return to Albania. I did not want to lose my friends in Greece.
>
> (GR-10)

> At first it sounds like a joke, but finally I realized that they were serious. My father wanted to return and invest in Albania and be close to his family, to his relatives. My reaction was a bit strange – 50 per cent of themselves wanted to return and the other 50 per cent did not want to. I knew I would miss Italy.
>
> (IT-02)

Some households adopted a phased return: the parents and younger children moved back to Albania as worsening socio-economic conditions made their stay impossible, while adolescent children stayed behind with family until finishing school, then joined their parents and younger siblings in Albania. Some families first moved within the host country in search of employment, albeit without success.

> I was born in Athens after my parents moved from Patras to Athens. I lived in Athens until the sixth grade. Then we moved to Kavala and I stayed there until the end of high school. My father decided to move to Kavala following my uncle's advice who told him that things were better in Kavala. For the last three years my father did not have much work and he had some problems with his documents. Then my parents took the decision to temporary return to Albania in order to test the situation there. They took my younger brother with them and left me in Kavala so that I could finish the high school. So I stayed with my uncle 'til I finished my high school and then returned to Lushnja.
>
> (GR-05)

> My father's employment contract expired and he returned to Albania, so I lived alone in Italy for a few months. I lived with relatives there but without my family. My family left and I was left

alone so I decided to return. My parents did not want me to return. They told me 'what are you going to do in Albania?'.

(IT-05)

These testimonies point to the dynamic nature of return as well as to the importance of return preparedness (Cassarino 2014). In order to understand the decision-making process that precedes return, one should unfold both the motivations behind the decision and the strategies followed to realize it. While the decision-making can be highly contextual and contingent upon specific circumstances, the macro drivers that influence it are structural and related to discrimination in host countries; reduced career prospects or better study opportunities shape the more personal, family-level decisions.

Returning 'for good'

At this point, a key question is whether our returnees have acted independently (i.e. leaving their parents behind or acting against their will), or are they returning as part of a family return migration set forth by their parents?

The fact is that half of our (adult) respondents (eight out of 16), especially those coming from Greece (six out of ten), said that the decision to return and relocate (i.e. temporary) to their parents' homeland was fairly individual and taken independently. In similar studies (Christou 2006; King and Christou 2008; Vathi 2011) the return journey is seen under the light of the 'counter-diasporic migration' of second-generation youth (King and Christou 2010), while the first generation remains in the host country (Vathi 2011). In contrast to that trend, other studies (King and Kılınc 2014; King, Christou and Ahrens 2011; Reynolds 2008) found a 'family-return route' or the 'family narrative of return' to prevail over individual decisions to return. However, it should be acknowledged beforehand that in spite of commonalities (among case studies), there are important differences in terms of gender and age of return (teenager or adult); ethnic origin and sense of belonging; cultural/religious specificities and identity formation; the nature of bilateral relations between (non-EU) countries involved (i.e. Greece–Albania; Germany–Turkey); geographical proximity that could facilitate back-and-forth mobility; and push-and-pull factors shaping the multiplicity of mobility channels.

What is even more intriguing is the question of why and how they decided to move to their parents' home country – a country far less wealthy than Greece and Italy, of which they had no prior experience of living in and to which they felt less attachment than to Greece or Italy. Given the fact that most of the interviewees are university students, the aspiration was one of upward mobility in both attaining graduate and post-graduate education and better career prospects, which was not achievable in Greece and Italy (or elsewhere).

Drawing on independently-returning respondents' narratives, we distinguish four main types of return. Of course, those types are not mutually exclusive since some respondents articulated more than one reason behind their decision to return, expected outcomes, and expectations.

Return for educational and employment reasons

This type of return is guided by the need to attend university as either an undergraduate or transfer student. Going to university for most Albanian families in Greece and Italy is viewed as a 'life-stage event' (King et al. 2011: 483). Respondents often viewed the route back to Albania via education channels as a means of academic or professional upward mobility and self-realization. Obviously, this largely stems from the difficulties accessing higher education in Greece or pursuing certain professions in both Greece and Italy.

> I gave university exams test (πανελλήνιες) and due to family pressure I chose a direction that I did not like, as a result of which I did not write well in the exams. So I started looking for universities in Albania and I liked English literature. My mom was not negative. My dad didn't want to allow me to go Albania, but I finally convinced him.
> (GR-03)

> I gave university exams test (πανελλήνιες) and passed to a TEI in Messolonghi. But due to the financial situation my parents couldn't cover the tuition fees. So I had made the decision to go to Albania. There were some options for studying abroad and among them was Albania. We also have a house in Albania which reduced the studies' costs as I wouldn't have to pay rent. I would also have my own relatives close by.
> (GR-04)

For its part, Albania has allowed for a kind of transnational education system provided by international universities – some of which are affiliated to American, Turkish, Greek, and Italian educational institutions – offering studies in English. As seen above, this results in the 'counter-diasporic migration' of second-generation youth (King and Christou 2010), while the first generation remains in the host country (Vathi 2011: 351).

> I was born in the city of Puke, Albania, and I went to Greece when I was eight months. My father is an oil painter and my mother is currently looking after a lady. They both live in Greece. Only I moved to Albania to study.
>
> (GR-08)

A smaller number of respondents embarked on a temporary and circular return journey to balance the situation of job precariousness back in Italy. Some sought professional advancement through jobs requiring higher qualifications (even if less well-paid) in order to access a different job market not available to them in Italy.

> Since my father's death I have been moving back and forth for the last five-six years for work reasons. Albania was the only country I could return and have my own house. I returned back to Italy in summer for seasonal work in collecting fruit. I work there from August 'til November. When back to Albania I worked in a 'call centre' using my Italian language. It is in my interest to work Italy even seasonally. The salary of a month in Albania corresponds to two days work back in Italy.
>
> (IT-06)

Return as a journey of self-discovery and self-realization

The 'search for self' is a term employed by King et al. (2011) to illustrate this journey of return to the parents' homeland (ibid.: 483). This trend seems to be primarily a female storyline, with respondents experiencing it as a journey towards adulthood. Yet, their narratives revealed their intention to free themselves by severing ties with their families and social environment back in Greece and Italy – in some cases to escape traumatic events, an oppressive family environment, or disillusionment with their status in host countries.

> It was my idea. My parents were negative; there was no case for them. They did not want me to return to Albania. They wanted me to stay in Greece. They told me 'now that you got the Greek passport are you returning to Albania', 'everyone comes to Greece and you return to Albania'. I could not stand the idea. When you are upset with some people, with a place, you want to leave at all

costs. It was more like a personal revolution against the fact that my parents decided everything on my behalf. My mom freaked out when she heard about Albania.

(GR-06)

As illustrated above, our respondents generally projected return as an individual and independent decision, either as something planned over a period of years, perhaps built on favourable experiences accumulated during holiday visits, or as something that developed more spontaneously, with the return seen as an adventurous endeavour.

It had been two years since I had decided to return to Albania. During that time I often visited Albania and had a really good time. Then it stuck in my mind the idea of studying here and I returned. It was a whim. I wanted to live and enjoy my 'home' (τόπος). Overall, I wanted a change in my life.

(GR-08)

Return for personal/intimate and familial reasons

This type of return is projected as an act of reuniting with a partner or related to marriage, with more women involved in this type of return. It can also be a means to reunite with the nuclear or extended family in Albania and is related to lifestyle preferences.

It was not so much for the studies because there it would be better and free but more because of my relationship. I thought that if I studied in Italy, I would lose my partner. My family was not very happy with this decision as every parent wants something much better for their child than to return to Albania. But in the end they supported me.

(IT-03)

Return as a 'way out' strategy from downward mobility

In this type of return, return migration to their parents' homeland enacts a 'way out' scheme representing an alternative route to achieving upward mobility through opportunities respondents felt were denied to them living in Greece and Italy.

Before returning to Albania we [he and his brother] were thinking about different scenarios. It was either to move to any other area within the Italian territory or go to another country. We made some efforts but the point is that I had to renovate my resident permit every year and I was not allowed to move anywhere else. Therefore every plan to go somewhere else was useless. I even consulted a lawyer who told me that the only way was to have an indefinite contract (*indeterminata*). But in the given circumstances of crisis it was difficult even to find a job and let alone to find a person who could provide for me an indefinite contract.

(IT-06)

These four types of 'return' to the parental homeland have a gendered dimension that is particularly interesting. Some young women (IT-03; IT-05; GR-05) return to reunite with their partner or spouse or families while others undertake return independently, almost as an act of defiance or self-realization (GR-03; GR-04; GR-06; GR-08). Clearly the age of our respondents is important: being in their late adolescent years or early 20s, they are faced with important life-stage events that prompt them to make a decision to stay, return, or leave for third countries.

Interestingly, dual citizenship has contributed to the emergence of a new type of return, 'temporary return' (Khadria 2010: 186). This newly intensified temporary return or otherwise called circulatory migration is an expression of fluid mobilities that constitute a 'lesson taught' when it comes policies towards dual citizenship, particularly in the context of the migration and development. In fact, holding a Greek or Italian passport – that is, EU citizenship – the temporary return of second-generation Albanians could then be further extended to make possible even multilateral mobilities within the EU in which they are eligible to reside under the status of EU citizen.

In sum, the attitude towards return has primarily developed through a transnational understanding and evaluation of opportunities in both home and host country thus also shedding light on prevailing integration patterns in Greece and Italy (Vathi 2015). As such, the findings offer significant evidence on how return does not constitute the end of a migration cycle but instead is part of transnational system entailing a matrix of social, cultural, and economic relationships whose dynamics cut across countries, cultures, and societies. Finally, the picture gleaned from respondents is that of increasingly predetermined, well-planned, and adequately organized journey of return that can be characterized as intrinsically context-based. This corroborates the findings of Michail and Christou (2016) that second-generation Albanians act in a more calculating self-preservation mode of survival than an emotionalized pursuit of ethnic membership (ibid.: 10).

(Re)-integration in the parental homeland

In the scholarly literature, the integration of returnees in the homeland is coupled with the 4Rs: 'repatriation, reintegration, rehabilitation, and reconstruction' (Lippman and Malik 2004; Kuschminder 2017: 8). For obvious reasons, the return and reintegration of second-generation 'returnees' follows a different path. Indicative terms for such a process would be those of 'adjustment' (Christou 2006), 'integration' (Kuschminder 2017), or 'adoption' (Vathi and Duci 2016). Those terms, indeed, touch upon the core elements of the second generation's return to their parents' homeland.

Going beyond the micro-level approach, in his study on return migration Cassarino (2004) stresses the relevance of contextual and situational factors linked to return migration. This is even more relevant in the case of the second generation, where, unlike their parents, the young returnees have no experience of living in the reality of their parents' homeland and are unfamiliar with the country's socio-political system. Such situational factors can only be evaluated in a post-return phase when the experience of 'adjustment' affecting everyday life can be objectively evaluated and measured (Cassarino 2004: 5; Gmelch 1980: 143).

Experience and available information about life in Albania is usually based on family narratives and short visits, which, in turn, do not help create an accurate portrayal of the life in the country of origin. In addition, for those second-generation returnees forced to live in rural areas or even in cities in peripheral locations, the project of 'return' is doomed to failure. Thus, for return to be a viable and sustainable scenario for second-generation returnees, it can only be effective through the settlement in a larger urban environment such as Tirana and Durres where they could feel more 'at home'.

> As soon as I saw the situation in Elbasan I moved to Tirana together with my mother. We have rented a house.
>
> (IT-01)

> After return we were accommodated to the city of Lezha, to my paternal home. I could not live there. Using my studies as an occasion, I moved to Tirana.
>
> (GR-10)

Integration upon return is intrinsically linked to issues of belongingness and identity (Vathi and Duci 2016). Second-generation returnees' values and emotions relate to their Greek or Italian socialization, creating what Lulle (2017) has labelled 'cosmopolitan geographies' of young people. For their return to be sustainable, this liminality or linkage with both countries has to be acknowledged and negotiated. This is not an easy journey because young returnees may feel alien to the parental homeland and marginalized:

> Albanians do not understand some things. They prejudge you. I do not like this. I can't stand others interfering with my life.
> (GR-08)

These difficulties can be compounded by their age and life stage. Xhesi returned to Albania in 2016, at the age of 19; she believes her decision to leave Italy was the biggest mistake of her life.

> Even today I cannot reintegrate into Albanian society. I had a lot of difficulties with the recognition of the Italian diploma; I had a very difficult time. I also started working long hours and I suffered from anorexia for a few months. With the support of my parents I quit the job and began studying Law at the university.
> (IT-05)

Kristi, born and raised in northern Greece, feels integrated in Albania by socializing with peers of the same age who also grew up in Greece. It's Kastoria, her native city in Greece, she sees as home:

> I have found people who make me feel at home. They are also the girls who are from Greece, we share the same view, and we also speak Greek. It's a little easier.
> (GR-06)

The process of negotiating return is dependent on personal and familial circumstances. For Bledi (a young boy born in Slovakia and raised in Italy), returning to Albania after a troubled adolescence in Italy and the death of his father there has triggered a new start, a journey to adulthood.

> I like the fact that Albanians are a little more serious as people, more fanatical and protective for their families. Here, I became a bit more responsible and down to earth person.
>
> (IT-01)

For those returnees still in high school, return could be challenging as they had difficulties in adjusting to the Albanian education system; they did not speak as fluently, the curricula differ, and teachers pointed to their gaps. This was often experienced as culture shock and led to a decline in their educational performance (Vathi et al. 2016: 12).

> I knew nothing about Albanian literature. I could read but I could not do exercises or homework. So, my teacher told me to start with a lower level, with a seventh-grade book, while I was in the eighth grade.
>
> (GR-02)

While macro factors like the educational system and intercultural education policies (or the absence thereof) structure the return experience of teenagers still at school, navigating the situation had more to do with their social environment and personal skills, or the resources they could mobilize.

With regard to the young returnees' human capital, the lack of linguistic skills in Albanian was a major drawback:

> The language made it more difficult for me. As soon as I realized that there were other girls from Greece, I breathe a sigh of relief, as I would communicate with at least one person. I have a problem with Albanian dialects. As originally being from the north it is difficult to communicate even with people from central or southern Albania.
>
> (GR-03)

But there was a small group of second-generation returnees who mobilized social and human capital acquired at the destination country and used that to succeed in their reintegration in Albania. The case of Maria is telling in this respect. She easily found a job in a call centre working for a company in Italy. Her knowledge of Italian thus became an asset and her poor Albanian was no longer an issue. Besides her fluency in Italian, Maria could mobilize her knowledge of Italian culture, customs, and colloquial expressions.

> Last year I start working in a call centre where I used my Italian. Salaries in relation to the public sector are very good. Now as a student I work six hours in the afternoons.
> (IT-03)

> I managed to find a job in a call centre and so I felt myself superior to others because I knew I had the experience of Italy, its language, lifestyle, education, and other certain aspects.
> (IT-05)

Mobility as a way of life

The return process is conceptualized as a continuum of experiences unfolded at different stages, including post-return mobilities and remigration (Vathi 2017). In some studies (for instance, Bivand Erdal and Oeppen 2017) post-return mobilities are considered key to the wellbeing of returnees by making the country of origin an 'alternative home'. In this sense, 'home' could be either here or there, or simultaneously here and there, providing that migrants are rational 'players' whose choices are shaped by economic factors, mobility resources, and emotional necessities (Bivand Erdal 2014: 367–379). Some of our interviewees had this experience of transnationalism, having lived in three countries like Bledi mentioned above:

> My parents initially went to Bratislava with my sisters and I was born there. Six months later we moved to Taranto, Italy. Eighteen years later, my mother and I returned to Albania and my sisters are married to Italians and live in Taranto.
> (IT-01)

As also shown by Porobic (2017), the transnational mobilities of Bosnian returnees were a coping strategy of households seeking satisfactory life conditions after return. Porobic talks about open-ended returns consisting of transgenerational and transnational homemaking in different places and countries in order to optimize the outcomes of migration. As illustrated below, there are cases whereby the family's experience with migration seems to inspire a more mobile attitude towards the second generation's future life and ideas of settlement.

Migration becomes a form of life in pursuit of better education or career prospects or in seeking better living conditions. The existence of transnational family ties is important as both cultural (mentality) and social (networks) capital.

> My brother has remigrated to Germany and lives permanently there with my dad now. They live in Germany with my uncle. My brother has a Greek passport and has signed a contract with a football club. Mom has been left alone in Greece. And my sister has returned to Albania.
>
> (GR-03)

In such cases transnational living becomes the norm, either as an ongoing lifestyle or for specific periods of time (Bivand Erdal et al. 2016: 845)

> My sister is married to an Albanian and they live in Greece. They do not have in mind the scenario of return. But they want to go somewhere abroad and they have some friends in Britain.
>
> (GR-07)

Given the dynamics of transnational space and mobilities among the second generation, some scholars have taken a further step by suggesting that the term 'second generation' is replaced with 'transnational generation', with the latter encompassing second generation in both the homeland and the new land (Levitt and Waters 2002; Glick Schiller and Fouron 2001; Levitt and Glick Schiller 2004).

At the same time, fostering a transnational life might be a reaction to or coping strategy against the deregularization, discrimination, and downward socio-economic mobility experienced in the host country (Wessendorf 2013; Ambrosetti, Cela, and Fokkema 2013). Nonetheless return is seen more as a stage in a mobile livelihood rather than as a final destination.

> Neither in Albania nor in Greece. I like Greece because my parents are there and my house is there too, but not for work. I have not decided yet but I once I complete my Bachelor [degree] I want to go somewhere in an English spoken country. I do not exclude also Germany and Austria.
>
> (GR-09)

Onward migration to a third country further compounds the transnational ties of the second generation. Karamoschou's (2018) study of Albanian second-generation respondents who left Greece to move to the UK offers interesting insights. Faced with Brexit and the risk of losing their EU citizenship status in the UK, young second-generation Greek Albanians indicate that they will return to Greece rather than Albania (King and Karamoschou 2019: 165).

Concluding remarks

This chapter has reviewed the return and remigration or onward mobility experience of second-generation youth in Albania who were born or raised (or both) in Greece or Italy. The chapter's central aim has been to map the different types of 'return' for this second generation and particularly the ways in which such 'return' resembles or differs from that of their parents.

Our analysis has shown that the return decision for this second generation is clearly affected by the impact of the economic crisis in Greece and Italy on themselves and their families by altering their life, education, and employment prospects. Particularly for those who were not highly skilled or whose families were less affluent in Greece or Italy, the recession's impact was dramatic and pushed them to unprepared return, as was the case with their parents (Chapter 3). Like first-generation returnees, these respondents' degree of agency in their return decision depended largely on macro-level factors like unemployment rates and migration policies leading to their families and themselves losing their legal status at destination.

The second generation's choices, of course, were also limited by age and life stage. Those younger than 18 had little say in the overall decision and often simply followed their parents, while those who returned as young adults were still significantly constrained by the overall circumstances as they had barely finished their studies or landed their first job. At the same time their life stage offered them the opportunity to consider return to Albania or onward migration as a new option for life.

Focusing on their motivations and their making sense of their 'return', we have identified four types of return/onward mobility: for education, for employment, for emotional reasons, and as a resilience strategy counteracting downwards socio-economic mobility. Whether return is more utilitarian (job, school) or symbolic (making a new beginning, rediscovering the homeland of their parents), our second-generation returnees show a high level of adaptability and resilience mobilizing their cultural and social resources from both origin and destination countries. They navigate available opportunities, turning their migration experience into an asset, even though many testify to ugly and harsh discrimination and stigmatization experiences in the country of destination. But rather than choosing between the two countries, our interviews testify to the existence of a 'transnational space' that these young second-generation returnees navigate. This transnational space does not only include Greece or Italy and Albania but also third countries to which they have transnational family ties, in which they may have lived, or to which they may aspire to emigrate. While they are acutely aware of their identity and the experiences of exclusion they faced growing up, they are also particularly flexible in connecting and blurring the 'here' and 'there', 'origin' and 'destination'. This shows that it may indeed be meaningless to speak about this second generation as returning 'home' because the sense of 'belonging' to a country may no longer be the overarching aspiration and a state of hybrid identity is perceived as a desirable condition (Cairns et al. 2014: 4).

Summarizing, while the first generation attempts to reconcile rupture from choosing between places that they made their home and their country of origin or migrating to a new country, the second generation is adopting a hybrid identity. Many of the latter are technically Albanian because that is the origin of their parents, but they were born, raised, and socialized according to Greek or Italian cultural norms and values. To them, Albania means belonging to their parents' homeland while returning to their family roots (Wessendorf 2007: 1097). But, once in Albania, they feel trapped in a place which they once hoped would be their home but where they feel like strangers. Interestingly, as this study has shown, a significant number of second-generation Albanian migrants cast doubt on their ethnic attachment to Albania, Italy, and Greece; instead, a cosmopolitan identity seems to prevail (Gemi 2019: 116).

References

Alba, R. and Nee, V. (2003) *Remaking the American Mainstream: Assimilation and Contemporary Immigration*. Cambridge, MA: Harvard University Press.

Ambrosetti, E., Cela, E. and Fokkema, T. (2013) The Differential Impact of the Legal Status of Migrants in Italy on Transnationalism: Just a Matter of Time and Integration? *Journal of Mediterranean Studies* 22 (1), 33–60.

Andall, J. (2002) Second-Generation Attitude? African-Italians in Milan. *Journal of Ethnic and Migration Studies*, 28 (3), 389–407.

Athanasopoulou, A. (2007) *Family Debts, Personal Desires and Migratory Realities: Albanian Second-Generation Youth in Athens*. Paper presented at the EAPS working group 'Beyond National Boundaries', 13–14 December.

Berthoud, R. (2000) *Family Formation in Multi-cultural Britain: Three Patterns of Diversity*. ISER Working Paper. Colchester: University of Essex.

Bhabha, H. (1990) Interview with Homi Bhabha: The Third Space. In: Rutherford, J. (ed.) *Identity: Community, Culture and Difference*. London: Lawrence and Wishart, pp. 207–221.

Bivand Erdal, M. (2014) 'This is My Home'. Pakistani and Polish Migrants' Return Considerations as Articulations About 'Home'. *CMS*, 3 (3), 361–384.

Bivand Erdal, M., Amjad, A., Zaman Bodla, Q, Rubab, A. (2016) Going Back to Pakistan for Education? The Interplay of Return Mobilities, Education, and Transnational Living. *Population, Space and Place*, 22, 836–848.

Bivand Erdal, M. and Oeppen, C. (2013) Migrant Balancing Acts: Understanding the Interactions Between Integration and Transnationalism. *Journal of Ethnic and Migration Studies*, 39 (6), 867–884.

Bivand Erdal, M. and Oeppen, C. (2017) Forced to Leave? The Discursive and Analytical Significance of Describing Migration as Forced and Voluntary. *Journal of Ethnic and Migration Studies*, 44 (6), 981–998.

Boyd, M. (2002) Educational Attainments of Immigrant Offspring: Success or Segmented Assimilation? *International Migration Review*, 36 (4), 826–875.

Brubaker, R. (1992) *Citizenship and Nationhood in France and Germany*. Cambridge, MA: Harvard University Press.

Cairns, D., Sardinha, J. and Tiesler, N.C. (2014) *Mapping the Return Migration Research Field*. CIES e-Working Paper No. 197/2014. Lisbon: Centre for Research and Studies in Sociology, ISCTE-University of Lisbon.

Casacchia, O. (2007). *Studiare insieme, crescere insieme? Un'indagine sulle seconde generazioni in dieci regioni italiane*. Milan: Edizione Franco Angeli.

Cassarino, J. P. (2004) Theorising Return Migration: The Conceptual Approach to Return Migrants Revisited. *International Journal on Multicultural Societies* 6 (2), 253–279.

Castles, S. and Miller, M. (2003) *The Age of Migration*. New York: Guilford Press.

Cavounidis, J. (2018). The Migration Experience of Greece and the Impact of the Economic Crisis on its Migrant and Native Populations. *European Journal of Public Health*, 28 (Supplement 5), 20–23.

Cavounidis, J. and Cholezas, I. (2013) Educational and Labour Market Trajectories of Youth of Migrant Origin. Available at: www.kepe.gr/images/meletes/

STUDIES_75_Cavounidis_Cholezas_educational_and_labour_market_trajec tories_of_youth_of_migrant_origin.pdf [Accessed 8 September 2020]. [in Greek]
Cela, E. (2017) Migration and Return Migration in Later Life to Albania: The Pendulum between Subjective Wellbeing and Place. In: Vathi, Z. and King, R. (eds) *Return Migration and Psychosocial Wellbeing: Discourses, Policy-Making and Outcomes for Migrants and their Families.* Abingdon: Routledge, pp. 203–220.
Chatzidaki, A. and Maligkoudi, C. (2012) Family Language Policies among Albanian Immigrants in Greece. *International Journal of Bilingual Education and Bilingualism*, 16 (6), 675–689.
Chatzidaki A. and Xenikaki, I. (2012) Language Choice among Albanian Immigrant Adolescents in Greece: The Effect of the Interlocutor's Generation. *Menon*, 1, 4–16.
Child, I. L. (1943) *Italian or American? The Second Generation in Conflict.* New Haven, CT, Yale University Press.
Chimienti, M., Bloch, A., Ossipow, L. and Wihtol de Wenden, C. (2019) Second Generation from Refugee Backgrounds in Europe. *Comparative Migration Studies*, 7 (40).
Christou, A. (2006) *Narratives of Place, Culture and Identity: Second-Generation Greek-Americans Return 'Home'.* Amsterdam: Amsterdam University Press.
Clifford, J. (1994) Diasporas. *Cultural Anthropology*, 9 (3), 302–338.
Clough Marinaro, I. and Walston, J. (2010) Italy's 'Second Generations': The Sons and Daughters of Migrants. The American University of Rome, *Bulletin of Italian Politics*, 2 (1), 5–19.
Crul, M. and Vermeulen, H. (2003) The Second Generation in Europe. *International Migration Review*, 37 (4), 965–986.
Da Cruz, M. (2018) Offshore Migrant Workers: Return Migrants in Mexico's English-Speaking Call Centers. *The Russell Sage Foundation Journal of the Social Sciences*, 4 (1), 39–57.
Elliot, A. (2009) *Legal, Social and Intimate Belonging: Moroccan and Albanian Second-Generation Migrants in Italy.* UCL-WPN, Working Paper No. 05/2009. London: University College London.
Farley, R. and Alba, R. (2002) The New Second Generation in the United States. *International Migration Review*, 36 (3), 669–701.
Frisina, A. (2007) *Giovani musulmani d'Italia.* Rome: Carocci Editore.
Garcés-Mascareñas, B. and Penninx, R. (2016) *Integration Processes and Policies in Europe: Contexts, Levels and Actors.* IMISCOE research series. Berlin: Springer.
Gemi, E. (2016) Integration and Transnational Mobility in Time of Crisis: The Case of Albanians in Greece and Italy. *Studi Emigrazione*, LIII (202), 237–255.
Gemi, E. (2019) *Integration and Transnationalism in a Comparative Perspective: The Case of Albanian Immigrants in Vienna and Athens.* Vienna: Verlag der Österreichischen Akademie der Wissenschaften.
Gkaintartzi, A., Kiliari, A., and Tsokalidou, R. (2014) 'Invisible' Bilingualism – 'Invisible' Language Ideologies: Greek Teachers' Attitudes towards

Immigrant Pupils' Heritage Languages. *International Journal of Bilingual Education and Bilingualism*, 18 (1), 60–72.

Glick Schiller, N. and Fouron, G. (2001) I Am Not a Problem without a Solution: Poverty, Transnational Migration, and Struggle. In: Good, J. and Maskovsky, J. (eds) *New Poverty Studies: The Ethnography of Politics, Policy and Impoverished People in the US*. New York: New York University Press, pp. 321–362.

Gmelch, G. (1980) Return Migration. *Annual Review of Anthropology*, 9, 135–159.

Gogonas, N. (2010) *Bilingualism and Multiculturalism in Greek Education*. Newcastle upon Tyne: Cambridge Scholars.

Gogonas, N. and Michail, D. (2014) Ethnolinguistic Vitality, Language Use and Social Integration amongst Albanian Immigrants in Greece. *Journal of Multilingual and Multicultural Development*, 36 (2), 198–211.

Gordon, M. M. (1964) *Assimilation in American Life: The Role of Race, Religion, and National Origins*. New York: Oxford University Press.

Hirschman, C. (2001) The Educational Enrollment of Immigrant Youth: A Test of the Segmented-Assimilation Hypothesis. *Demography*, 38, 317–336.

Hoxha-Laro, D. (2012). Reintegration of the Children of the Returnee Emigrants in the Albanian Educational System. *Journal of Educational and Social Research*, 2 (5), 175–178.

Iliadis, C. (2014) Citizenship in Greece Impossibility for the Second Generation of Migrants: New Faces Conference Paper German Council on Foreign Relations. Available at: https://dgap.org/en/research/publications/citizenship-greece-impossible-citizenship [Accessed 8 September 2020].

Joppke, C. (1999) *Immigration and the Nation State: The United States, Germany, and Great Britain*. Oxford: Oxford University Press.

Jurado, E. (2008) Citizenship: Tool or Reward? The Role of Citizenship Policy in the Process of Integration. Policy Network Paper. Available at: www.policy-network.net/uploadedFiles/Publications/Publications/Citizenship_tool_or_reward.pdf [Accessed 8 September 2020].

Karamoschou, C. (2018) *The Albanian Second Migration: Albanians Fleeing the Greek Crisis and Onward Migrating to the UK*. Sussex Centre for Migration Research Working Paper no. 93. Brighton: University of Sussex.

Khadria, B. (2010) Adversary Analysis and the Quest for Global Development: Optimizing the Dynamic Conflict of Interest in Transnational Migration. In: Glick Schiller, N. and Faist, T. (eds) *Migration, Development, and Transnationalization: A Critical Stance*. New York: Berghahn Books, pp. 176–203.

Kibria, N. (2002) *Becoming Asian American: Second-Generation Chinese and Korean American Identities*. Baltimore, MD: Johns Hopkins University Press.

Kılınc, N. (2014) *Second-Generation Turkish-Germans Return 'Home': Gendered Narratives of (Re-)negotiated Identities*. Sussex Centre for Migration Research Working Paper no. 78. Brighton: University of Sussex.

King, R. (2011) Geography and Migration Studies: Retrospect and Prospect. *Population, Space and Place* 18, pp. 134–153.
King, R. and Christou, A. (2008) *Cultural Geographies of Counter-Diasporic Migration: The Second Generation Returns 'Home'*. Sussex Migration Working Paper no. 45. Brighton: University of Sussex.
King, R. and Christou, A. (2010) Cultural Geographies of Counter-diasporic Migration: Perspectives from the Study of Second-Generation 'Returnees' to Greece. *Population, Space and Place*, 16 (2), 103–119.
King, R., Christou, A., and Ahrens J. (2011) 'Diverse Mobilities': Second-Generation Greek-Germans Engage with the Homeland as Children and as Adults. *Mobilities*, 6 (4), 483–501.
King, R. and Karamoschou, C. (2019) Fragmented and Fluid Mobilities: The Role of Onward Migration in the New Map of Europe and the Balkans. *Migracijske i etničke teme*, 35 (2).
King, R. and Kılınc, N. (2014) RoutesTo Roots: Second-Generation Turks from Germany 'Return' to Turkey. *Nordic Journal of Migration Research*, 4 (3), 126–133.
King, R. and Kılınc, N. (2016) The Counter-Diasporic Migration of Turkish-Germans to Turkey: Gendered Narratives of Home and Belonging. In: Nadler, R., Kovács, Z., Glorius, B., and Lang, T. (eds) *Return Migration and Regional Development in Europe. Mobility Against the Stream*. Basingstoke: Palgrave Macmillan, pp 167–194.
King, R. and Mai, M. (2004) Albanian Immigrants in Lecce and Modena: Narratives of Rejection, Survival and Integration. *Population, Space and Place* 10 (6), 455–477.
Kokkali, I. (2011) Migrant Strategies and Modes of Adaptation of Albanian Immigrants in the Greek Society. In: Moïsidis. A. and Papadopoulou, D. (eds) *The Social Integration of Third-Country Nationals in the Greek Society*. Athens: Kritiki Editions [in Greek].
Koopmans, R., Statham, P., Giugni, M., and Passy, F. (2005) *Contested Citizenship: Immigration and Cultural Diversity in Europe*. Minnesota, MN: University of Minnesota Press.
Kuschminder, K. (2017) *Reintegration Strategies: Conceptualizing How ReturnMigrants Reintegrate*. Basingstoke: Palgrave Macmillan.
Levitt, P. and Glick Schiller, N. (2004) Conceptualizing Simultaneity: A Transnational Social Field Perspective on Society. *ZMR*, 38 (3), 1002–1039.
Levitt, P. and Waters, M. (2002) *Changing Face of Home, The: The Transnational Lives of the Second Generation*. New York: Russell Sage Foundation.
Lippman, B. and Malik, S. (2004) The 4Rs: The Way Ahead? *Forced Migration Review*, 21, 9–11. Available at: www.africabib.org/htp.php?RID=P00033283 [Accessed 8 September 2020].
Lulle, A. (2017) The Need to Belong: Latvian Youth Returns as Dialogic Work. In: Vathi, Z. and Kind, R. (eds) *Return Migration and Psychosocial Wellbeing Discourses, Policy-Making and Outcomes for Migrants and their Families*. Abingdon: Routledge.

Louie, V. (2006) Second-Generation Pessimism and Optimism: How Chinese and Dominicans Understand Education and Mobility Through Ethnic and Transnational Orientations. *International Migration Review*, 40 (3), 537–572.

Mai, N. (2011) *Reluctant Circularities: The Interplay between Integration: Return and Circular Migration within the Albanian Migration to Italy*. Florence: European University Institute.

Mai, N. and Paladini, C. (2013) Flexible Circularities: Integration, Return and Socio-Economic Instability within the Albanian Migration to Italy. In: Triandafyllidou, A. (ed) *Circular Migration Between Europe and its Neighbourhood*. Oxford: Oxford University Press, pp. 42–68.

Mai, N. and Schwandner-Sievers, S. (2003) Albanian Migration and New Transnationalisms. *Journal of Ethnic and Migration Studies*, 29 (6), 939–948.

Malson, H., Marshall, H., and Woolleett, A. (2002) Talking of Taste: A Discourse Analytic Exploration of Young Women's Gendered and Racialized Subjectivities in British Urban, Multicultural Contexts. *Feminism & Psychology*, 12 (4), 469–490.

Maroukis, T. (2012) *Update Report Greece: The Number of Irregular Migrants in Greece at the End of 2010 and 2011*. Clandestino Database on Irregular Migration. Athens: ELIAMEP.

Maroukis, T. and Gemi, E. (2013) Circular Migration between Greece and Albania: Beyond the State? In: Triandafyllidou A. (ed.) *Circular Migration between Europe and its Neighbourhood: Choice or Necessity*. Oxford: Oxford University Press, pp. 68–89.

Michail, D. (2010) Language Maintenance/Shift among Second Generation Albanian Immigrants in Greece: Social Integration and Mobility. *Ethnologia* 14, 207–224 [In Greek].

Michail, D. (2013) Social Development and Transnational Households: Resilience and Motivation for Albanian Immigrants in Greece in the Era of Economic Crisis. *Southeast European and Black Sea Studies*, 13 (2), 265–279.

Michail, D. and Christou, A. (2016) Diasporic Youth Identities of Uncertainty and Hope: Second-Generation Albanian Experiences of Transnational Mobility in an Era of Economic Crisis in Greece, *Journal of Youth*, 19 (7), 957–972.

Michail, D. and Christou, A. (2018) Youth Mobilities, Crisis, and Agency in Greece: Second Generation Lives in Liminal Spaces and Austere Times. *Transnational Social Review: A Social Work Journal*, 8 (3), 245–257.

Paladini, C. (2014) Circular Migration and New Forms of Citizenship. The Albanian Community's Redefinition of Social Inclusion Patterns. *European Journal of Research on Education*, 2 (6), 109–115.

Porobic, S. (2017) 'Invisible' Returns of Bosnian Refugees and Their Psychosocial Wellbeing. In: Vathi, Z. and King, R. (eds) *Return Migration and Psychosocial Wellbeing: Discourses, Policymaking and Outcomes for Migrants and their Families*. Abingdon: Routledge, pp. 108–125.

Portes, A., Guarnizo, L. E., and Landolt, P. (1999) The Study of Transnationalism: Pitfalls and Promise of an Emergent Research Field. *Ethnic and racial studies* 22 (2), 217–237.

Portes, A. and Rumbaut, R. (2001) *Legacies: The Story of the Immigrant Second Generation*. Berkeley, CA: University of California Press.

Portes, A. and Zhou, M. (1993) The New Second Generation: Segmented Assimilation and Its Variants among Post-1965 Immigrant Youth. *Annals of the American Academy of Political and Social Science*, 530, 74–98.

Reynolds, T. (2008) *Ties That Bind: Families, Social Capital and Caribbean Second-Generation Return Migration Families & Social Capital*. Research Group Working Paper No. 23. Brighton: University of Sussex, Sussex Centre for Migration Research.

Rumbaut, R. G. (1997) Paradoxes (and Orthodoxies) of Assimilation. *Sociological Perspectives*, 40 (3), 483–511.

Rumbaut, R. G. (2004) Ages, Life Stages, and Generational Cohorts: Decomposing the Immigrant First and Second Generations in the United States. *International Migration Review*, 38 (3), 1160–1205.

Sansone, L. (1995) The Making of a Black Youth Culture: Lower-Class Young Men of Surinamese Origin in Amsterdam. In: Amit-Talai, V. and Wulff, H. (eds) *Youth Cultures: A Cross-Cultural Perspective*. London, Routledge, pp. 114–143.

Sardinha, J. (2011) Returning Second-Generation Portuguese-Canadians and Portuguese-French: Motivations and Senses of Belonging. *Journal of Mediterranean Studies* 20 (2), 231–254.

Schierup, C. U., Hansen, P. and Castles, S. (2006) *Migration, Citizenship, and European Welfare State: A European Dilemma*. Oxford: Oxford University Press.

Teerling, J. (2011) The Development of New 'Third-Cultural Spaces of Belonging': British-Born Cypriot 'Return' Migrants in Cyprus. *Journal of Ethnic and Migration Studies*, 37 (7), 1079–1099.

Thomson, M. and Crul, M. (2007) The Second Generation in Europe and the United States: How is the Transatlantic Debate Relevant for Further Research on the European Second Generation? *Journal of Ethnic and Migration Studies*, 33 (7), 1025–1041.

Tsaliki, L. (2011) Mediations of Europe's Others: Representations of Albanian Immigrants in the Greek Media. In: Sarikakis, K. and Lodge, J. (eds) *Communication, Mediation and Culture in the Making Europe*. Bologna: Il Mulino, pp. 82–105.

Thurairajah, K. (2017) The case of the Sri Lankan Tamil diaspora and homeland: A shared ethnic identity? *Studies in Ethnicity and Nationalism*, 17 (1), 115–132.

Triandafyllidou, A. (2007) Mediterranean Migrations: Problems and Prospects for Greece and Italy in the Twenty-first Century. *Mediterranean Politics*, 12 (1), 79–86.

Triandafyllidou, A., Gropas, R., and Isaakyan, I. (2015) *Transnational Mobility, Human Capital Transfers and Migrant Integration*, ITHACA project, Policy Paper, October. Florence: European University Institute. Available at: https://cadmus.eui.eu/handle/1814/37984 [Accessed 8 September 2020].

Vathi, Z. (2009) *New Brits? Narratives of Migration and Settlement of the Albanian-Origin Immigrants in London*. Paper presented at IMISCOE Annual Conference, Stockholm.

Vathi, Z. (2011) A Context Issue? Comparing the Attitude Towards Return of the Albanian First and Second Generation in Europe. *Journal of Mediterranean Studies*, 20 (2), 343–364.

Vathi, Z. (2015) *Migrating and Settling in a Mobile World: Albanian Migrants and Their Children in Europe*. IMISCOE Research Series. Berlin: Springer.

Vathi, Z. (2017) The Interface between Return Migration and Psychosocial Wellbeing. In: Vathi, Z. and Kind, R. (eds) *Return Migration and Psychosocial Wellbeing Discourses, Policy-Making and Outcomes for Migrants and their Families*. Abingdon: Routledge, pp. 1–18.

Vathi, Z. and Duci, V. (2016) Making Other Dreams: The Impact of Migration on the Psychosocial Wellbeing of Albanian-Origin Children upon Their Families' Return to Albania. *Childhood*, 23 (1), 53–68.

Vathi, Z., Duci, V. and Dhembo, E. (2016) Homeland (Dis)integration: Educational Experience, Children and Return Migration to Albania. *International Migration* 54 (3), 159–172.

Vathi, Z., Duci, V. and Dhembo, E. (2019) Social Protection and Return Migration: Trans-national and Trans-temporal Developmental Gaps in the Albania-Greece Migration Corridor. *Migration and Development*, 8 (2), 243–263.

Vathi, Z. and King, R. (eds) (2017) *Return Migration and Psychosocial Wellbeing: Discourses, Policymaking and Outcomes for Migrants and their Families*. Abingdon: Routledge.

Vertovec, S. (1997) Three Meanings of 'Diaspora' Exemplified among South Asian Religions. *Diaspora*, 6 (3), 277–299.

Waldinger, R. (2007) *Between Here and There: How Attached Are Latino Immigrants to Their Native Country?* Washington, DC: Pew Hispanic Center.

Waldinger, R. and Feliciano, C. (2004) Will the New Second Generation Experience 'Downward Assimilation'? Segmented Assimilation Re-assessed. *Ethnic and Racial Studies*, 27 (3), 376–402.

Wessendorf, S. (2007) 'Roots Migrants' Transnationalism and 'Return' among Second Generation Italians in Switzerland. *Journal of Ethnic and Migration Studies*, 33 (7), 1083–1102.

Wessendorf, S. (2013) Commonplace Diversity and the 'Ethos of Mixing': Perceptions of Difference in a London Neighbourhood. *Identities, Global Studies in Culture and Power*, 20 (4), 407–422.

Wihtol de Wenden, C. (2005) Multiculturalism in France. *Canadian Diversity*, 4 (1), 68–73.

Zincone, G. and Basili, M. (2009) Country Report: Italy. EUDO Citizenship Observatory, RSCAS, EUDO-CIT-CR 2009/01. Available at: http://eudo-citizenship.eu/docs/CountryReports/Italy.pdf [Accessed 8 September 2020].

Zinn, D. L. (2005) The Second Generation of Albanians in Matera: The Italian Experience and Prospects for Future Ties to the Homeland. *Journal of Southern Europe and the Balkans*, 7 (2), 259–277.

5 A typology of return, reintegration, and onward mobility

Introduction

This book has studied the return, reintegration, and onward or circular mobility patterns among first- and second-generation Albanian citizens who spent time in Italy and Greece and returned to Albania during the 2010s. We have theoretically conceptualized and analytically investigated return not as the final stage of their migration project but rather as one leg of a long and complex journey. We have sought to bring together our analysis of the macro factors that structure the southeastern European migration system constituted by Albania, Italy, and Greece – notably the historical, social, economic, and political linkages among these countries – with the meso factors (local and transnational networks and a 'culture' of migration) while focusing on the micro-level of individuals and their households.

Our study follows other recent research that has sought to disentangle the links between (successful) return and reintegration, arguing that the two ought to be considered as distinct (King 2017; Kuschminder 2017a, 2017b) and that sustainable return does not necessarily mean that the migrant and their family will not engage into new migration. The proximity and close ties among the three countries has provided a privileged space from which to analyse circularity between the former destination country and the origin country and to show how return can be coupled with significant transnational mobility. Our delving into the experiences of both first-generation returnees and second-generation children who had to 'return' to their parents' homeland sheds light on the dynamic, effectively volatile, nature of return. Building on the insights on return and remigration in southeastern Europe (Loizou et al. 2014; Maroukis and Gemi 2013; King 2018) we looked at preparedness (for return) and reintegration as two processes that 'frame' return, which is preceded by preparedness and followed by reintegration. Both preparing for return and reintegrating shape further decisions of staying in the country of origin, circulating to the former country of immigration, or remigrating to a new destination.

The book draws on extensive fieldwork conducted between 2014 and 2017, notably several years after the onset of the 2008 financial crisis. This timeframe allowed us to capture both the aftermath of the crisis and the gradual improvement of economic conditions in all three countries and in Europe overall. The book draws on 67 qualitative interviews in several Albanian cities. The interviews brought together factual information about return and remigration but also looked at how the interviewees made sense of their migration project and how they took decisions and mobilized resources whether to return, remigrate, reintegrate, or circulate as strategies of survival, resilience, or indeed further upwards mobility. Our qualitative micro-level investigation is informed by our analysis of the macro-level factors (employment, household structure, wider economic conditions, and relevant labour, migration and welfare policies at origin and destination), and the meso-level elements (specific contextual factors such as networking with co-ethnics and locals at destination and with family and friends at origin, professional networks, access to support by civil society or state institutions, and a certain culture of migration).

This chapter compares the drivers for return, the types of return and post-return mobilities in which migrants engage, and their reintegration or onward migration challenges between first-generation and second-generation returnees. First-generation migrants include those Albanian citizens who migrated to Italy or Greece as adults after having grown up in the country of origin, while the second generation includes those who were born in the destination country or moved there as very young children, went to school there, but in late adolescence or young adulthood had to return to Albania along with their parents. The chapter concludes by proposing a typology of return, reintegration, and mobility that emerges from the findings of this research.

Drivers of return

Albanian return migration to Greece and Italy in the 2010s was largely triggered by the Eurozone crisis of 2009 which left many migrants unemployed or underemployed. An overwhelming majority of our interviewees (40 out of 51) clearly stated that the crisis was a major exogenous factor that altered their plans and prompted them to consider returning to Albania. For several households there was a domino effect caused by unemployment, particularly of the husband and father. Not only did they lose the household's main source of income, but they also lost their legal status; those who did not possess a long-term permit were unable to renew their papers without an active job offer. For many returning to Albania was not part of their plans:

> If the crisis had not happened ... I would never have returned to Albania.
>
> (IT-5)

This was the case even if they had repaired the family home or maintained ties with the country:

> We went on vacation in Albania once a year ... Apart from our family homes, we did not purchase any property and we did not think about any investment there. Our life was in Greece.
>
> (GR-18)

While the impact of the crisis was significant for all interviewees, it was experienced differently. Some felt it as a negative driver for return, while for others this sudden downward socio-economic mobility was a bulwark for starting anew in Albania. Many had repaired their houses, bought a shop, or had savings that they could put to fruition. They thus saw this as an opportunity as well as an act of resilience. Instead of resigning themselves to their fate, they acted to change it:

> We said, we have money, we know the job. So why are we not going to open something of our own [in Albania].
>
> (GR-20)

Others, however, spent their savings in the hope that things would improve and found themselves obliged to return when they ran out of money and living in Greece became impossible. The turning point for these returnees too was often an opportunity, notably a job offer in Albania through a relative or during a holiday. Often in these cases the decision was made by the husband and father:

> My brother-in-law introduced my husband to a contractor who hired him for a construction work. He accepted immediately. He made the decision on behalf of all of us without asking me first.
>
> (GR-18)

Among our first-generation interviewees there were only two who spoke about return as an option among many, neither positive nor necessarily negative (GR-14 and GR-25). For them, both single men who had lived in Greece for more than 18 years (in Thessaloniki and Athens respectively), return came at a phase in their lives where a decision to marry tipped the balance towards going back to Albania and starting a new life there. This sense of return as a stage in one's life is, by contrast, frequently encountered among our second-generation interviewees. Returning to Albania for them could be an education opportunity (going to college or university there) but also a sense of trying something new and different, a small revolution against the will of their parents:

> It was my idea. My parents were negative ... They did not want me to return to Albania ... It was more like a personal revolution against the fact that my parents decided everything on my behalf. My mom freaked out when she heard about [it].
>
> (GR-06)

Half of our second-generation respondents who were adults at the time of moving back to Albania (notably 8 out of 16 interviewees) took the decision to return fairly independently. However, the other half – and particularly those who were still adolescents at the time of returning – did not have a chance to decide for themselves; the decision was taken by their parents because of economic hardship and unemployment or because the whole family lost their legal status:

> At first it sounds like a joke but finally I realized that they were serious. My father wanted to return and invest in Albanian, and be close to his family, to his relatives.
>
> (IT-02)

Our study shows that while the decision to return is dominated by macro factors such as the economic crisis and consequent unemployment and loss of income or legal status, the meso factors such as networks are crucial for the individual migrant and their family to take the decision and make the move. It is at the micro level of individual decision and action and the meso level of mediating factors where return's contours are shaped as opportunity or forced decision.

Types of return

Analysing the types of returns of first- and second-generation returnees, three patterns clearly emerge in this order of importance:

permanent return; transnational return and onward mobility; and occasional return or circularity between the two countries.

Permanent return was the largest category among our first-generation interviewees, with approximately half (25 interviewees) stating that their return to Albania was for good. For those who had prepared for return by making investments and mobilizing networks to find employment or start a small business in Albania, the long-term return plan was the obvious choice. In these cases, return involved establishing one's own small business or setting up the children to enrol in university. However, the same was true for a large part of those who had been pushed to an abrupt return – this was the case for 20 out of the 25 permanent returnees – despite the difficulties. At the same time, in those who were pushed to return with little preparedness, there was constant re-evaluation of the options, drawing into question whether the return was permanent or temporary:

> At the moment, when we returned, we did not know yet whether we were coming back permanently or temporarily.
>
> (IT 12)

> If I do not achieve something here, I am thinking of returning to Greece again.
>
> (GR-3)

Twenty per cent of our interviewees opted for occasional or circular return as a survival strategy. They basically followed the employment opportunities, and in these cases the family usually resettled in Albania and the husband and father circulated between the two countries working seasonal jobs in agriculture and construction. This pattern is also adopted by some second-generation returnees who follow in the circular footsteps of their parents:

> Since I was 15 years of age, I have been working in the summers in Greece ... Every summer I go to Greece and work in a bar.
>
> (GR-07)

Nearly one-third of the individuals interviewed engaged in temporary return to Albania, while living transnationally with family members divided between the main country of origin and destination (notably Albania and Italy or Greece) or engaging in onward mobility to a third country like Germany or Austria. This type of temporary return was not a survival strategy chasing employment opportunities but was rather developed as a family plan aimed at upwards socio-economic or educational mobility. Such transnational family life and complex mobility could be part of a wider plan to repay a loan for a house bought in Italy or Greece or to allow for children to complete their education at the former destination country (whether Italy or Greece) while the parents relocated to Albania.

In other cases, though, the long-term plan was to ensure a good education for their children – at a good private school that they could afford:

> my parents enrolled my sister to a school in Albania, Arsakeio, to get a recognized diploma. So my sister had already returned to Albania and that was the reason for us to return.
>
> (GR-02)

This could also involve mobility towards a third country:

> My brother is two years older than me ... He is in Bucharest, he is studying [medicine] ... My parents are in Greece while I am here in Albania studying at the university.
>
> (GR-01)

The patterns of temporary return and onward transnational mobility typically spread over two or three generations within the same family involving the first-generation migrants as parents or grandparents and the second-generation returnees as children or parents also themselves. The driver of this transnational mobility pattern of the entire family relates to employment opportunities more often than not:

> My brother has remigrated to Germany and lives permanently there with my dad now ... Mom has been left alone in Greece. And my sister has returned to Albania.
>
> (GR-03)

These findings corroborate the results of other recent research on the transnational mobility of returnees, such as that of Porobic (2017) on Bosnians or Karamoschou (2018) on Albanian second-generation youth studying in the UK.

Overall the type of return is conditioned by the preparation stages and the individual desires and aims of the returnees as well as their forward-looking plans. Remigration or onward mobility to a third country, whether for education or employment, is taken up by many families as part of a wider plan to build a better future through mobility. Thus, return becomes only one stage in this longer plan, and it appears that the previous migration experience (and the human, social, and material capital accumulated through it) becomes the lever for developing a new transnational living.

Reintegration challenges and opportunities

Turning our focus to the reintegration challenges faced by our interviewees, there are some significant differences emerging that are also related to the stage of life in which each of the two generations faces return and with their previous experience in Albania or their ties to it. Thus, while the first generation knows the language and local traditions and has strong familial ties at the country of origin, the second generation often struggles to be accepted, whether at school or in the workplace. At the same time, first-generation returnees feel greater responsibility and urgency to make a living and build a better future in Albania for themselves and their children. However, both groups emphasize the differences and discrepancies between their two 'lives' and how they have to negotiate their sense of belonging either here or there.

The accounts of reintegration challenges and opportunities among the first-generation returnees focus more on their disappointment with the way the public administration works and the importance of having strong network support and knowing people. At the same time, they also point to the competitive edge that their transnational experience and professional networks in the destination country (whether Italy or Greece) provides them. Their grievances concern concrete problems like poor infrastructure, corruption, or poor service quality in Albania more than with feelings of being rejected by fellow nationals, even if as one informant notes:

> Upon return you just realize that you have been missing for a long time ... You are claiming your position from the beginning. Returning is never easy.
>
> (GR-26)

For second-generation returnees while practical reintegration challenges such as speaking and writing Albanian correctly and reintegrating into high school are also important, their transnational cultural capital appears to be more of an advantage if they can mobilize it to make friends among other returnees (GR-06) or when, for instance, knowledge of the Italian language can become an important employment asset for working at a call centre (IT-03 and IT-05).

Our informants also emphasize the countryside vs urban centres divide that can be relatively pronounced in Albania; several returnees point to the difficulty of reintegrating in smaller towns and feeling more at home in Tirana (IT-01 and GR-10). Others though note that in Tirana they feel a double rejection – as returnees from abroad and as people who come from the countryside ('provincial' in the sense of backwards):

> I feel like a dual stranger. First, because I am the Greek and secondly because I am a "provincial". I have never seen more racism for the "provincials" than in Tirana ... The "Tiranians" call [the "provincials"] "Chechens", meaning uncivilized.
>
> (GR-25)

Indeed, our findings suggest that reintegration does not happen in a homogenous environment of the 'homeland' but rather in specific local contexts – in smaller cities or in the capital, at school or at work – and the previous migration experience is both an asset and a liability. Here, individual agency and mobilizing networks are crucial in negotiating both social and economic reintegration. Feelings of alienation can arise nonetheless among both second-generation and first-generation migrants.

Developing a typology of return, reintegration, and mobility

Building on both the relevant literature and our findings in this study, we propose a new typology of return, reintegration, and onward mobility that places return in the middle of the migration experience rather than at its endpoint and seeks to connect the dots of preparedness, type of return, level of reintegration, and type of remigration or onward mobility.

Over half a century, a wide range of studies have tried to explore and explain the multiple factors shaping migrants' patterns of return and reintegration (Cassarino 2014: 159). As far as return is concerned, some typologies are based on the levels of development of countries linked by migration and return as for instance from less developed countries to highly developed ones, while other migration moves may include 'ancestral' return rather than return of migrants (King 2000: 10). Additional typologies distinguish between intended behaviour and the eventual migration outcome (Bovenkerk 1974: 10) and the historical evolution of the migration process and level of acculturation in the country of destination (Cerase 1974).[1]

132 *A typology of return migration*

The typology suggested by Gmelch (1980) draws on three types of return migrants: (1) temporary migrants, that is, returnees who intended temporary migration; (b) forced returnees, that is, returnees who intended permanent migration but were forced to return; and (c) voluntary returnees, that is, returnees who intended permanent migration but chose to return. Yet many scholars have questioned to what degree this is actually a voluntary return. Cassarino (2008) poses this in another way, asking if this form of return is *decided* or *compelled?* Decided return refers to those who '*chose on their own initiative to return, without any pressure or coercion*', whereas compelled return refers to someone '*who returns to his/her country of origin as a result of unfavourable circumstances and factors which abruptly interrupt the migration cycle*' (ibid.: 113)

The last and most relevant typology proposed by King (2017: 8) is based on the length of time that migrants spend in the country of origin. It includes four types of return patterns:

1 occasional returns (i.e. short-term or/and periodic visits);
2 periodic/seasonal/circular returns (i.e. seasonal/circular work activities);
3 temporary returns (i.e. returns for a period but with intention to re-migrate); and
4 permanent return (i.e. people returning to the home country for good).

On the other hand, the reintegration typologies share the basic assumption that migrants' patterns of reintegration are shaped by three interrelated elements:

1 context in home countries (place);
2 the duration and type of migration experience lived abroad (time); and
3 the factors or conditions in the host and home countries that motivated return (pre- and post-return conditions) (Cassarino 2014: 159).

However, Cassarino supports the theory that a basic condition connecting any person who returns home from abroad is the level of return preparedness. Even though Cassarino does not clearly engage with the notion of migrant agency and how migrants seek to take control of their life, his analysis speaks directly to that level of individual (and household) agency mobilizing resources and navigating related policy options and surrounding conditions (Triandafyllidou 2019).

The notion of r*esource mobilization* is particularly relevant here as it refers to tangible (primarily economic) as well as intangible resources (social networks, knowledge and ideas) which can be used during the migration experience, and also includes resources migrants drew upon, such as their social capital, prior to the migration project (Cassarino 2014: 15). *Preparedness* refers to both migrants' willingness to return as well as the degree to which they are economically and psychologically ready to do so. Cassarino draws on a typology based on three categories of returnees distinguished by levels of preparedness: high, low, and non-existent. In terms of reintegration, according to Gmelch (1980) there are two ways to assess it: first, by examining the actual economic and social conditions of returnees and, second, by focusing on migrants' own perceptions.

In proposing a tailor-made typology arising from our research, we also consider some additional elements, notably the continuum of duration-intention and the motivation (subjectively and objectively assessed) of returning. With regard to the former, it is quite impossible to study return migration without first considering the emigration factors (Bovenkerk 1974: 9). The most important question here is: was the emigration meant as permanent or only as a temporary migration? Relevant to our case is the fact that whether migrants decide to stay or plan to return is sometimes not so much decided by themselves but rather by *force majeure*. For instance, in the case of an Albanian migrant who intended to stay permanently in Greece or Italy, they were forced to return by a deterioration of economic status, unemployment, and discriminatory legislation. As regards the latter, notably the motivation for returning, it is important to distinguish whether returnees subjectively assess their migration project as a success or failure, regardless of whether they voluntarily decided to return. This relates to Cassarino's point as regards decided vs compelled voluntary return (Cassarino 2014). Following from the above reflections, we propose a typology of return, reintegration, and further mobility that takes into account the type of return, the level of preparedness, the level of reintegration, and the chosen type of mobility after return (Table 5.1).

While significantly influenced by exogenous factors such as the acute economic crisis that affected both Greece and Italy in the early 2010s, Albanian first- and second-generation returnees developed a variety of patterns of return and reintegration and actively shaped their livelihoods with significant vivacity and resilience. Their experiences clearly

134 *A typology of return migration*

Table 5.1 Typology of return migration, re-integration, and mobility

Category	Type of return	Level of preparedness	Level of re-integration	Mobility		Re-migration
				Transnational/circular		
1	occasional return	Non-existent	Non-existent – refusal	Existent – directed towards other countries		Existent scenario, dependant on legal status or/ and social networks
2	periodic/ seasonal/ circular return	Partially existent depending on circumstances	Partially existent – depending on social networks Lack of access to labour market in country of origin	High level of mobility for seasonal/circular employment in tourism and agricultural sectors		Partially existent – to industrial countries of EU (Germany, UK) and USA – Dependent on age and family composition.
3	Temporary return	Low level of preparedness because of interrupted and incomplete migration cycle	Low level of re-integration because the lack of willingness and preparedness, as well as the structural exclusion in Albania	Not very articulated – transnational activities are limited to family transfers		Re-migration to EU, USA, Canada
4	Permanent return	Medium to high level of preparedness	Low to medium level mainly due to proper activization of social networks in absence of re-integration policies and opportunity structures	Transnational activities are limited to family transfers, individual projects, study		Re-migration if conditions are favourable

suggest that return today is only a phase of migration, that reintegration is a process that is linked to but at the same time also separate from the decision to stay in the country of origin permanently or engage into remigration or onward migration. Such decision and subsequent action are not final and can be renegotiated as the experience of migration and return appears to create a significant transnational capital – a propensity towards mobility and an intimacy with transnational living that facilitates onward movement. Indeed, Albanian return migration in the 2010s is typically a migration of the twenty-first-century: dynamic and open-ended.

Note

1 Cerase distinguished four types of return among Italians migrants in the USA: (a) return of failure; (b) return of conservatism; (c) return of innovation; and (d) return of retirement.

References

Bovenkerk, F. (1974) *The Sociology of Return Migration: A Bibliographic Essay.* The Hague: Martinus Nijhoff.

Cassarino, J. P. (ed.) (2008) *Return Migrants to the Maghreb Countries Reintegration and Development Challenges.* MIREM Project General Report. Florence: European University Institute. Available at: www.jeanpierrecassarino.com/wp-content/uploads/2011/12/MIREM-_General_Report_2008.pdf [Accessed 8 September 2020].

Cassarino, J. P. (2014) *A Case for Return Preparedness. In: Battistella, G. (ed.) Global and Asian Perspectives on International Migration.* Global Migration Issues 4. Berlin: Springer, pp. 153–166.

Cerase, F. (1974). Expectations and Reality: A Case Study of Return Migration from the United States to Southern Italy. *The International Migration Review,* 8 (2), 245–262.

Gmelch, G. (1980) Return Migration. *Annual Review of Anthropology,* 9, 135–159.

Karamoschou, C. (2018) *The Albanian Second Migration: Albanians Fleeing the Greek Crisis and Onward Migrating to the UK.* Sussex Centre for Migration Research Working Paper no. 93. Brighton: University of Sussex.

King, R. (2000) Generalization from the History of Return Migration. In IOM (ed.) *Return Migration: Journey of Hope or Despair?* Geneva: United Nations. pp 7–55.

King, R. (2017) *Return Migration and Development: Theoretical Perspectives and Insights from the Albanian Experience.* Keynote lecture to the 2nd Annual Conference of the Western Balkans Migration Network – 'Migration in the Western Balkans: What Do We Know?', Sarajevo, 19–20 May.

King R. (2018) Is Migration a Form of Development Aid Given by Poor to Rich Countries? *Journal of Intercultural Studies*, 39 (2), 114–128.

Kuschminder, K. (2017a) *Reintegration Strategies: Conceptualizing How Return Migrants Reintegrate*. London: Palgrave Macmillan.

Kuscminder, K. (2017b) Interrogating the Relationship between Remigration and Sustainable Return. *International Migration*, 55 (6), 107–121.

Loizou, E., Michailidis, A., and Karasavvoglou, A. (2014). Return Migration: Evidence from a Reception Country with a Short Migration History. *European Urban and Regional Studies*, 21 (2), 161–174.

Maroukis, T. and Gemi, E. (2013) Albanian Circular Migration in Greece: Beyond the State? In: Triandafyllidou, A. (ed.) *Circular Migration between Europe and its Neighbourhood: Choice or Necessity?* Oxford: Oxford University Press, pp. 68–90.

Porobic, S. (2017) 'Invisible' Returns of Bosnian Refugees and Their Psychosocial Wellbeing. In: Vathi, Z. and King, R. (eds) *Return Migration and Psychosocial Wellbeing: Discourses, Policymaking and Outcomes for Migrants and their Families*. Abingdon: Routledge, pp. 108–125.

Triandafyllidou, A. (2019) The Migration Archipelago: Social Navigation and Migrant Agency. *International Migration*, 57 (1), 5–19.

List of interviewees returned from Italy, 2014–2017

ala	Interviewee's code	Date of interview	Place of interview	Nationality	Gender (M/F)	Age	Educational level	Family status	Year of return	Years of stay in GR/IT
1	01-IT	9/2/2014	Shkoder	Albanian	M	50	University	Married	2010	13
2	02-IT	17/2/2014	Shkoder	Albanian	M	29	Secondary	Married	2012	7
3	03-IT	17/2/2014	Shkoder	Albanian	F	36	University	Married	2011	7
4	04-IT	17/2/2014	Shkoder	Albanian	M	42	Secondary	Married	2011	17
5	05-IT	17/2/2014	Shkoder	Albanian	M	51	Secondary	Married	2013	14
6	06-IT	18/2/2014	Shkoder	Albanian	F	40	University	Married	2013	20
7	07-IT	18/2/2014	Shkoder	Albanian	M	43	Secondary	Married	2010	8
8	08-IT	18/2/2014	Shkoder - Italy (video-call)	Albanian	F	49	Secondary	Married	2011	18
9	09-IT	19/2/2014	Lezhe	Albanian	M	33	Compulsory education	Married	2011	13
10	10-IT	24/2/2014	Tirane	Albanian	M	39	Compulsory education	Married	2013	15
11	11-IT	26/2/2014	Tirane	Albanian	M	34	University	Single	2012	11
12	12-IT	1/3/2014	Tirane	Albanian	M	48	University	Married	2012	14
13	13-IT	3/3/2014	Shkoder	Albanian	M	26	Secondary	Single	2013	17

a/a	Interviewee's code	Date of interview	Place of interview	Nationality	Gender (M/F)	Age	Educational level	Family status	Year of return	Years of stay in GR/IT
14	14-IT	3/3/2014	Shkoder	Albanian	M	23	University	Single	2013	4
15	15-IT	4/3/2014	Shkoder	Albanian	F	52	Secondary	Married	2013	16
16	16-IT	18/3/2017	Tirane	Albanian	F	36	Tertiary	Married	2016 (Nov)	14
17	17-IT	24/3/2017	Tirane	Albanian & Italian	M	63	Tertiary	Married	2016 (Jun)	25
18	18-IT	7/4/2017	Shkoder	Albanian	M	33	Secondary	Single	2013 (Jun)	7
19	19-IT	23/3/2017	Tirane	Albanian	M	36	Tertiary	Single	2016 (Sep)	17
20	20-IT	5/3/2017	Shkoder	Albanian	M	47	Tertiary	Married	2016 (Jul)	17
21	21-IT	7/4/2017	Shkoder	Albanian	F	31	University	Married	2015 (Oct)	5
22	22-IT	24/3/2017	Shkoder	Albanian	F	38	Secondary	Widow	2010	7 (returned to Albania 2010; remigrated to Italy 2016)
23	23-IT	28/4/2017	Tirane	Albanian	F	36	Tertiary	Married	2013 (Jun)	12
24	24-IT	4/4/2017	Fushe Kruje	Albanian	M	52	Elementary	Married	2015 (Aug)	21
25	25-IT	15/3/2017	Lezhe	Albanian	M	36	Secondary	Married	2012 (May)	15

List of interviewees returned from Greece, 2014–2017

ala	Interviewee's code	Date of interview	Place of interview	Language of interview	Gender (M/F)	Age	Educational level	Family status	Year of return	Years of stay in GR
1	01-GR	02/3/2014	Tirane	Albanian	M	49	Secondary	Married	2013 (Sep)	22
2	02-GR	02/3/2014	Tirane	Albanian	F	43	Secondary	Married	2013 (Sep)	15
3	03-GR	02/3/2014	Tirane	Albanian	F	44	Secondary	Married	2013 (Sep)	17
4	04-GR	3/3/2014	Shkoder	Albanian	F	50	Secondary	Married	2013	16
5	05-GR	4/3/2014	Tirane	Albanian	F	29	Secondary	Married	2013 (May)	17
6	06-GR	4/3/2014	Tirane	Albanian	M	55	Secondary	Married	2011	7
7	07-GR	4/3/2014	Shkoder	Albanian	M	47	Secondary	Married	2012 (Dec)	20
8	08-GR	8/03/2014	Tirane	Albanian	F	53	Secondary	Married	2013	18
9	09-GR	10/03/2014	Tirane	Albanian	M	45	Secondary	Married	2013	23
10	10-GR	10/03/2014	Tirane	Albanian	F	35	Secondary	Married	2013	23
11	11-GR	3/3/2014	Shkoder	Albanian	M	38	Secondary	Married	2012	18
12	12-GR	6/3/2014	Tirane	Albanian	M	38	Elementary	Married	2012	20

ala	Interviewee's code	Date of interview	Place of interview	Language of interview	Gender (M/F)	Age	Educational level	Family status	Year of return	Years of stay in GR
13	13-GR	3/3/2014	Shkoder	Albanian	M	44	Secondary	Married	2011 (Dec)	20
14	14-GR	8/3/2014	Tirane	Albanian	M	39	Higher education	Married	2012 (Jan)	20
15	15-GR	7/3/2014	Tirane	Albanian	F	63	University	Married	2013	21
16	16-GR	3/3/2014	Shkoder	Albanian	F	40	Secondary	Married	2012	15
17	17-GR	18/3/2017	Tirane	Albanian	F	40	Secondary	Married	2013 (Aug)	16
18	18-GR	3/4/2017	Lezhe	Albanian	F	43	Secondary	Married	2013 (Sep)	22 (returned to Greece in January 2019)
19	19-GR	23/3/2017	Tirane	Albanian & Greek	F	42	Secondary	Married	2016 (Oct)	25
20	20-GR	18/3/2017	Tirane	Albanian	M	50	Secondary	Married	2013 (Jul)	15
21	21-GR	25/4/2017	Tirane	Albanian & Greek	M	33	Tertiary	Single	2016 (Oct)	21 (18 in Greece; 3 in Sweden)

a/a	Interviewee's code	Date of interview	Place of interview	Language of interview	Gender (M/F)	Age	Educational level	Family status	Year of return	Years of stay in GR
22	22-GR	15/3/2017	Shkoder	Albanian	F	49	Tertiary	Married	2012 (Jun)	15
23	23-GR	15/3/2017	Shkoder	Albanian	F	42	Secondary	Married	2015 (Sep)	21
24	24-GR	22/4/2017	Tirane	Albanian	M	47	Tertiary	Married	2013 (Jun)	17
25	25-GR	22/4/2017	Tirane	Albanian	M	38	Secondary	Married	2014 (Mar)	17
26	26-GR	26/4/2017	Tirane	Albanian	M	62	Tertiary	Married	2014 (Apr)	23

Second-generation interviewees, Italy and Greece, 2017

a/a	Interviewee's code	Date of interview	Place of interview	Nationality	Gender (M/F)	Age	Status/educational level	Place of birth	Year of return	Years of stay in GR/IT
1	01-GR	13/03/2017	Tirane	Albanian	F	18	1st year university student	Albania (28 days old moved to Greece)	2016 (Sep)	17
2	02-GR	21/3/2017	Tirane	Albanian	M	16	Secondary	Heraklion, Crete, GR	2013 (Sep)	12
3	03-GR	20/3/2017	Tirane	Albanian & Greek	F	19	2nd year university student	Shkoder, Albania (2 years old moved to Greece)	2016 (Sep)	17
4	04-GR	15/3/2017	Tirane	Albanian & Greek (in 2016 got the citizenship)	F	22	Post-graduate studies	Elbasan, Albania (2 years old moved to Greece)	2013 (Jul)	16
5	05-GR	10/4/2017	Tirane	Albanian	F	18	1st year university student	Lushnje, Albania	2013 (Aug)	9

ala	Interviewee's code	Date of interview	Place of interview	Nationality	Gender (M/F)	Age	Status/educational level	Place of birth	Year of return	Years of stay in GR/IT
6	06-GR	26/4/2017	Tirane	Albanian & Greek	F	18	1st year university student	Kastoria, Greece	2016 (Oct)	17
7	07-GR	9/4/2017	Tirane	Albanian	M	20	2nd year university student	Fier, Albania (4 years old moved to Greece)	2011 (Jul)	12
8	08-GR	9/4/2017	Tirane	Albanian & Greek	F	20	2nd year university student	Puke, Albania (8 months old moved to Greece)	2014 (Jun)	17
9	09-GR	20/3/2017	Tirane	Albanian	F	20	2nd year university student	Elbasan, Albania (6 years old moved to Greece)	2014 (Sep)	13
10	10-GR	26/4/2017	Tirane	Albanian	M	24	Postgraduate student	Corfu, Greece	2013 (Jul)	20
11	01-IT	13/3/2017	Tirane	Albanian	M	26	Tertiary	Bratislava, Slovakia	2011 (Nov)	18
12	02-IT	15/3/2017	Tirane	Albanian & Italian	M	20	2nd year university student	Turin, Italy	2013 (Jun)	16

ala	Interviewee's code	Date of interview	Place of interview	Nationality	Gender (M/F)	Age	Status/educational level	Place of birth	Year of return	Years of stay in GR/IT
13	03-IT	17/4/2017	Tirane	Albanian	F	22	2nd year university student	Durres, Albania	2014 (Jun)	8
14	04-IT	22/4/2017	Tirane	Albanian	F	22	2nd year law student	Durres, Albania	2011 (Sep)	8
15	05-IT	26/4/2017	Tirane	Albanian	F	23	2nd year law student	Berat, Albania	2016 (Jul)	5
16	06-IT	3/3/2017	Shkoder	Albanian	M	29	Secondary	Shkoder, Albania	2014	17

Index

agency 11–16
Alba, R. 86
Albania 1, 4, 5, 14–17, 19, 24, 26, 29, 31, 32, 41, 51, 52, 54, 57, 64, 66, 74, 96–99, 101–3, 104–7, 124, 125, 126–7; *see also individual entries*
Albania–Italy–Greece migration system 7
Albanian citizens 1, 12, 18, 29, 30, 43, 67, 69, 74, 77, 78
Albanian migrants 12, 15, 16, 18, 19, 24–6, 28, 29, 45, 75, 76, 88–90
Albanian migration 12, 16–20, 26, 29, 48, 55, 64, 69, 70, 72, 75, 78; in Greece and Italy 26–32
Albanian return migration 13, 26, 31, 32, 45, 125, 133
Albanians 5, 7, 18, 19, 28, 29, 45, 49, 72, 83, 88, 93–101, 110–1
Andall, J. 84
assimilation 28
asymmetric assimilation 28

Baláž, V. 22
Balkans migration sub-system 16–20, 24
Biscione, A. 31
Bovenkerk, F. 20

capital investment 68
Carling, J. 49
Cassarino, J. P. 22, 23, 63, 87, 109, 131–3
Cena, E. 31
Child, I. L. 84

Christou, A. 25, 109
circular migration 46, 71–4
Clifford, J. 99
complexity approach 11
conflict theory approach 21
corruption 66
Crul, M. 84, 86
'cumulative causation' effect 14

differential exclusion 28, 89
differential inclusion 28
discrimination 53, 68, 85, 87, 93, 95, 97, 104
'disguised' identities 89–98
disintegration 84–98
Dragos, R. 65
dual citizenship 108

economic asylum seekers 29, 30
economic crisis 5, 7, 29, 52
economic refugeehood 12
economic reintegration 24
emotional cost–benefit 5
entrepreneurs 31
ethnic communities 14
Eurozone financial crisis 5, 13

family narrative of return 103–4; educational and employment reasons 105–6; personal/intimate and familial reasons 107; self-discovery and self-realization journey 106–7; 'way out' strategy, downward mobility 108–9
first-generation migrants 125

García-Pereiro, T. 31
Gëdeshi, I. 30, 55, 65, 74
Gemi, E. 51
gender distribution 43
gender inequalities 68
geographic proximity 27
Gmelch, G. 130, 131
Greece 1, 4, 5, 12–16, 26, 32, 41, 42, 48, 50–2, 54, 55, 61, 64, 66, 72, 73, 76, 77, 84, 87, 89, 91, 97, 123; Albanian migration in 26–32; migration system 7, 14, 16, 32

Haartsen, T. 25
Harris, J. R. 21
hybrid identities 83–115

INSTAT 7
intended permanent migration 130
IOM 7, 43
Italy 1, 4, 5, 12–16, 26, 32, 41, 42, 48, 51, 52, 55, 61, 64, 72, 73, 76, 77, 84, 87, 89, 90, 91, 92 Karamoschou 93, 124; Albanian migration in 26–32

Karamoschou, C. 88, 114, 129
Kazazi, B. 27
King, R. 16, 25, 27, 28, 30, 55, 65, 74, 88, 97, 106, 130
Koopmans, R. 97–8

Labrianidis, L. 27
Lee, E. S. 20
Lezha 7
life-cycle factors 53
Louie, V. 84
Lulle, A. 110

Macro factors 15
Mai, N. 28, 89, 97
massive emigration 12, 17, 18
meso-level factors 14–16, 24, 49, 52, 55
Michail, D. 108–9
migrant agency *see* agency
migrant decision-making 11, 12
migrant networks 13–16
migration 11–13; culture of 15, 16, 124; cycle 23, 26; drivers of 12;
flows 14, 16, 17; space 4; systems 1, 2, 4–8, 11–16, 22, 25, 32
mimesis 28
Morokvasic, M. 71

National Strategy for the Diaspora 69
National Strategy on Migration and its Action Plan 67
Nee, V. 86

onward migration 2–5
onward mobility 20–6, 31, 32, 41, 46, 50, 124, 126–9

Paladini, C. 31
partial integration 28
Porobic, S. 112
Portes, A. 84–6
post-return mobilities 69, 112, 125
poverty alleviation 64
preparedness 22–3, 25, 28, 31, 41, 45, 55, 56, 59, 60, 62, 123, 129, 131; level of 41, 55, 56, 62, 131; occasional, seasonal, and circular return 56–7; permanent return 59–63; return and levels of 55–6; temporary return and transnational mobility 57–9
protracted unemployment 29

quasi-organized migratory flows 14

Ravenstein, E. G. 20
readiness 22, 23, 31, 56
re-emigration 16, 20, 23, 24, 29, 31, 46, 62, 75, 76
Reiner, M. 65
re-integration 1–5, 7, 8, 11, 16, 19–26, 32, 41, 42, 67, 124–5, 129, 131; Albania 24, 64, 111; challenges and opportunities 7, 30, 63–9, 128–9; level of 23, 41, 129, 131; in parental homeland 109–12; patterns of 2, 24, 26, 63, 131; policies 42, 65; process 68, 88; typology 129–33
remigration 74–6
research methodology 6–7
resilience 12
resource mobilization 131

returnees 22, 26, 27, 30, 31, 42, 43, 45, 46, 54, 55, 65–8, 74, 77, 83, 129, 130, 131, 132
return migration 2–5, 20–6; flows 21; *see also* return mobilities
return mobilities 69; drivers 124–6; of first-generation Albanians 42–78; macro-, meso-, and micro-level drivers 48–50; negative drivers 50–3; pivotal drivers 53–4; positive drivers 54–5; seasonal and circular migration patterns 71–4; of second-generation migrants 83–115; trajectories of 98–104; transnational mobility and 69–71; types of returns 126–8; typology 129–33; way of life 112–14
return readiness 2

Schewel, K. 49
Schwandner-Sievers, S. 28
seasonal migration 71–4
second-generation Albanian migrants 88, 92, 96; second-generation Albanians 25, 95, 97, 98, 100, 108
second-generation (dis)integration 84–9
second-generation migrants 16, 83, 84, 86–8, 92
second-generation returnees 8
second-time emigration 20
self-employment venues 67
semi-structured interviews 6–7
Shkodra 7
Simon, H. A. 21
social alienation 68

social capital 5, 14
social insurance stamps 7
social networks 15, 22, 23, 56, 57, 75, 133, 134
social reintegration 24
socio-demographic profile 42–8
socio-economic integration 27
stigmatization 89–98, 115
subordinate integration 28

taxes 52
Thilo, L. 2
Thissen, F. 25
Tirana 66
Tirane 7
Todaro, M. P. 21
transnationalism approach 21
transnational mobility 23, 27, 32, 57, 58, 60, 69–71, 77, 83, 88, 124, 129
triangular migration system 1
typology 124–35

upward mobility 74, 85–7, 105, 107

Vathi, Zana 88, 89, 100, 101, 103
Vermeulen, H. 84, 86
Vullnetari, J. 27

William, A. 22
World Bank 64, 76

Xhaferaj, E. 30

Zhou, M. 84, 85
Zinn, D. L. 97

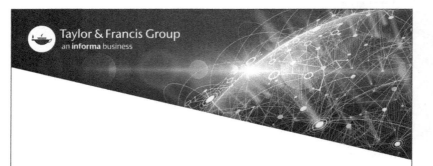